Everyday Law
for Immigrants

The Everyday Law Series

Edited by Richard Delgado and Jean Stefancic
University of Pittsburgh Law School

Everyday Law for Individuals with Disabilities
Ruth Colker and Adam Milani (2005)

Everyday Law for Children
David Herring (2006)

Everyday Law for Gays and Lesbians
Anthony C. Infanti (2007)

Everyday Law for Consumers
Michael L. Rustad (2007)

Everyday Law for Latino/as
Steven W. Bender, Raquel Aldana,
Gilbert Paul Carrasco, and Joaquin G. Avila (2008)

Everyday Law for Immigrants
Victor C. Romero (2009)

Forthcoming

Everyday Law for Women
April Cherry

Everyday Law for Seniors
Lawrence Frolik and Linda S. Whitton

Everyday Law for Patients
Alan Scheflin and A. Steven Frankel

Everyday Law for Immigrants

Victor C. Romero

Paradigm Publishers

Boulder • London

Copyright © 2009 Paradigm Publishers

Published in the United States by Paradigm Publishers, 3360 Mitchell Lane, Suite E, Boulder, CO 80301 USA.

Paradigm Publishers is the trade name of Birkenkamp & Company, LLC, Dean Birkenkamp, President and Publisher.

Library of Congress Cataloging-in-Publication Data
Romero, Victor C.
    Everyday law for immigrants / Victor C. Romero.
        p. cm. — (The everyday law series)
    Includes bibliographical references and index.
    ISBN 978-1-59451-627-6 (hardcover : alk. paper)
    ISBN 978-1-59451-628-3 (paperback : alk. paper)
    1. Emigration and immigration law—United States.   I. Title.
    KF4819.R663 2008
    342.7308'2—dc22

                                                                2008024313

Printed and bound in the United States of America on acid-free paper that meets the standards of the American National Standard for Permanence of Paper for Printed Library Materials.

Designed and typeset by: Mulberry Tree Enterprises

13   12   11   10   09   2   3   4   5

To Corie, Ryan, Julia, and Matthew

Contents

Acknowledgments

I am blessed to know many individuals who have graciously supported me during this project.

First and foremost, thanks to Richard Delgado and Jean Stefancic for inviting me to write this book for their Everyday Law series. Their contributions to the legal academy and to civil rights scholarship have been numerous and significant; their kindness and mentoring to me have been invaluable. Richard went the extra mile by reading early drafts of each chapter and providing detailed feedback. His keen editorial eye helped improve the manuscript tremendously. At Paradigm Publishers, thanks go to Beth Davis and Carol Smith for shepherding the project from start to finish with patience and thoughtfulness.

I am especially grateful to Won Kidane (Seattle University School of Law), Melissa Landrau-Rodriguez (Penn State's College Assistance Migrant Program), and Stephen Fotopulos (Tennessee Immigrant and Refugee Rights Coalition) for graciously reviewing an earlier draft of the book and steering me away from major errors or omissions. Insights from their tireless work on behalf of the migrants they serve helped me reexamine the issues afresh. Katrina Hall provided excellent research assistance by developing the charts and bibliography for the book; she also enjoys the dubious distinction of being my only research assistant with whom I have been able to converse in Tagalog. Cecily Giardina supplied useful information on accessing government resources in print and online. All errors that remain are, of course, mine alone.

Family, friends, and colleagues have provided other equally important sustenance. Phil McConnaughay, my dean at Penn State, has been particularly supportive of all my work. My colleagues in the Office of Academic Affairs at the law school gave me the flexibility to meet my deadlines. And my family in the Philippines and Singapore—Roberta and Roel, Georgy, Ben, Bets, and Billy—has been a constant source of strength and example of grace. I would be remiss if I did not mention the support of the Honorable David V. Kenyon, former U.S. District Judge of the Central District of California. Judge Kenyon was the first person who genuinely believed I could be a law teacher, and I will always be grateful for his encouragement.

Finally, and most important, I thank my wife, Corie Phillips Romero, and my kids, Ryan, Julia, and Matthew, for their patience during this long process. They all had to endure my occasional bouts of self-doubt as I slogged through the manuscript and publication process. Having adopted all three of our children from abroad and having immigrated myself, I am certain that our entire family would find our little sacrifice valuable if this book helps even a few readers better understand how we in America treat noncitizens in our midst.

Introduction

The United States has long been a nation of immigrants. From the Europeans who once thronged Ellis Island to the Asians who journeyed to Angel Island in the San Francisco Bay, people from all over the world have traveled to America for centuries in search of a new place to call home. Perhaps for just as long, the United States has responded to this migration with ambivalence, sometimes welcoming immigrants with open arms, other times seeking to return them to their places of birth. This schizophrenic attitude has led to a similarly schizophrenic immigration law history, one that reflects the tension between ensuring that immigrants assimilate into their adopted homeland and simultaneously protecting the interests of U.S. citizens and their nation.

In the tradition of other books in this series, *Everyday Law for Immigrants* aims to provide a comprehensive understanding of the basic challenges immigrants and foreign nationals face, not just within formal immigration policy (i.e., the law governing when noncitizens may enter, and must leave, the United States) but within U.S. domestic law generally, including rules promulgated by federal, state, and local entities that affect noncitizens (sometimes referred to as "alienage law"). This book aims to present a concise thematic overview of both historical and current U.S. immigration law and procedure while also answering alienage law questions of interest to noncitizens currently residing here, relating to topics such as employment and education. In short, I intend that noncitizens and their advocates will use this book not only to gain a bird's-eye view of U.S. immigration history, practice, and procedure but also to constructively address the many legal issues within immigration and alienage law that affect foreigners who reside here.

Despite its comprehensiveness, this book can only skim the surface when addressing the most common legal issues that affect noncitizens. Should your situation appear more complicated than the examples this book provides, you should seriously consider hiring a well-respected immigration attorney to assist you. A lawyer's help will go a long way toward ensuring that the information you have gleaned here is up-to-date and specifically applies to your unique circumstances.

Now, on to a detailed description of each chapter, and what I aim to accomplish.

Chapter 1 briefly outlines the history of U.S. immigration law and policy, setting forth both major congressional and U.S. Supreme Court activity. Immigration law encompasses the substantive and procedural rules that answer the questions, When may a noncitizen enter the United States? and When must that noncitizen leave? We will discover that, contrary to popular belief, immigration law is less about human rights than about the terms of a contract between the United States and noncitizens who wish to be here. Because the U.S. Constitution allocates power to the federal government to enact and enforce immigration law, the thrust of Chapter 1 will be to emphasize how the Supreme Court has essentially deferred to Congress's lawmaking authority over immigration law, only rarely intervening to curb that power and then doing so mostly through immigrant-friendly statutory interpretation rather than by appealing to unalienable constitutional rights. This so-called plenary power doctrine has allowed Congress to provide noncitizens, even longtime legal permanent residents, fewer protections under the Constitution's due process and equal protection clauses than it grants to U.S. citizens for similar discriminatory conduct. Fortunately, outside the realm of pure immigration law—within so-called alienage law—when individual state and local governments attempt to bar noncitizens by limiting their access to public goods and services, the Supreme Court has been more willing to protect noncitizens from governmental overreaching.

Thus, three themes emerge in this overview of constitutional immigration history: first, according to the Supreme Court's reading of the federal Constitution, Congress has virtually unlimited power to enact immigration policy, setting forth when noncitizens may enter and must leave the United States; noncitizens, therefore, have no *right* to be in the United States but are granted the *privilege* to reside here according to congressional will. Second, the U.S. Supreme Court has occasionally served as a check on congressional or presidential unfairness, affording a modicum of protection to noncitizens when the other branches of the federal government have overstepped the bounds of constitutional due process, or by narrowly interpreting anti-immigrant statutes in the noncitizens' favor. Finally, because Congress holds this broad power to enact immigration law, individual states and local governments do not; therefore, when states attempt to drive noncitizens from their territory by specifically targeting them based on their federal immigration status, the Supreme Court will step in to put an end to state discrimination; the only exception the Court has recognized is that states may limit certain government jobs to citizens when these occupations go to the heart of representative democracy.

Chapter 2 introduces the reader to the basics of immigration law — the rules that govern when noncitizens may enter, and when they must leave, the United States. Whereas Chapter 3 focuses on the procedures, Chapter 2 addresses the *reasons* why some noncitizens are admitted into the United States and why some others are deported. Specifically, we will learn that noncitizens are divided into two categories: those who intend to make the United States their home (immigrants), and those who are here temporarily for a specific purpose (nonimmigrants). Most people fail to understand this important distinction, which explains why students and tourists cannot make the United States their home while spouses of U.S. citizens can. In addition, Chapter 2 identifies the reasons why some noncitizens may be denied entry or be required to leave, as well as basic ways they may seek to overcome these reasons.

Chapter 3 provides a practical application of the history gleaned from Chapter 1 and the basic substantive immigration law learned from Chapter 2 by offering specific guidelines to best help solve a particular immigration problem. After opening with an introduction to how the federal immigration apparatus is structured and how it works, I will outline how one should approach immigration issues before delving into specific procedural steps one must take to solve an immigration problem. Unlike the U.S. criminal law system, immigration law is a civil law labyrinth administered by several complex agencies of the executive branch. As will be shown in Chapter 1, Congress has virtually unlimited power in enacting immigration law, and therefore, federal senators and congresspersons are usually good sources of help should immigration petitions get bogged down in red tape and the process need to be expedited. Where one is being adjudicated in the system, however—say, as a person awaiting deportation— Congress is more reluctant to intervene and prefers to let the administrative process run its course. It is therefore important to also be familiar with at least the most important procedural rules that help one navigate the murky waters of the immigration bureaucracy. The goal for Chapter 3, then, is for you to understand how immigration decisions get made, so that when you have an immigration problem you know where to turn. It is also hoped that the book will help you assess whether you are able to solve the issue on your own rather than seek help from an attorney.

Chapter 4 explores everyday civil rights issues that may affect foreign nationals aside and apart from their immigration woes. Put differently, this chapter switches from the focus in Chapters 2 and 3 on immigration law to alienage law: to those federal, state, and local government laws that affect the day-to-day life of noncitizens living in the United States. As an overview, this section will emphasize that, irrespective of Congress's plenary power over immigration law (as will be shown in Chapter 1), other federal, state, and local laws may provide noncitizens who are in the United States substantial protection. For example, although undocumented migrants are not exempt from the threat of deportation, if they should work, their employers are required to pay them the prevailing wage for their labor. The list of issues explored in the chapter is by no means exhaustive but is meant to provide applications of the general rule that outside immigration law, noncitizens may find some protection from favorable federal, state, and local alienage laws that may not immediately occur to them.

Chapter 5 lists useful resources, from websites and other online information to reference books and treatises.

1

Overview and History of U.S. Immigration Law

Immigration Policy as Contract Law

All nations distinguish between their citizens and others. In the United States, the law that creates these distinctions is found in immigration policy. The term *immigration law* refers to a rather narrow set of rules covering two aspects of a noncitizen's stay in the United States: first, those rules that govern when that noncitizen may enter, and second, those that dictate when he or she must leave. The whole of U.S. immigration law and policy relates to either of these two topics.

Although it is tempting to think of immigration law as primarily involving human rights (especially when we consider the protections afforded refugees), it is perhaps more accurate to view it as a form of contract law between the United States and the foreigner. The United States grants the noncitizen the privilege to enter the country for some specific purpose and amount of time, and, in exchange, the noncitizen promises to abide by the terms the country sets forth. Should the noncitizen breach his promise, he must leave the United States.

The Role of the Three Branches of the Federal Government in Immigration Law

The United States government consists of three branches—the legislature, the executive, and the judiciary—each of which plays a role in determining what the immigration laws mean, or, in keeping with the contract analogy, what responsibilities the state and the nonciti-zen have under the immigration contract. As the lawmaking body within the federal government, Congress has the responsibility for drafting the terms of the immigration contract between the United States and the noncitizens who seek entry. Like other federal laws, the terms of the contract are then executed and enforced by the pres-ident through administrative agencies such as the Department of Homeland Security, which promulgate specific regulations to en-force the broad terms of Congress's immigration policy. The U.S. Supreme Court, along with the lower federal courts, is charged with making sure that the terms of the contract are fairly enforced, using its interpretive skills to discern what Congress and the president had in mind when the laws and regulations governing a noncitizen's stay were drafted and whether these rules offend basic individual rights guaranteed by the Constitution.

Here is a quick example illustrating how the three federal branches create immigration policy together: Congress decides it is important for the United States to protect persons fleeing war-torn nations. It therefore passes a broad law setting forth a new category of immigrants—refugees—who may enter the United States under cer-tain conditions. The president is charged with implementing this gen-eral policy on a more specific, case-by-case basis. Let's say civil war breaks out in Jamaica and boatloads of Jamaicans board makeshift vessels in a desperate bid to make it to the Florida coast. Instead of waiting for the vessels to reach the United States, the president de-cides to send Coast Guard cutters carrying immigration inspectors to intercept the Jamaican boats. Upon interception, the immigration in-spectors board the vessels and begin efficiently screening the people on board to see if they qualify for refugee status under Congress's law. Some of the Jamaicans believe that the president's interception policy violates congressional intent, constitutional due process, or in-ternational law; accordingly, their lawyers sue the president, bringing the issue before the federal courts and perhaps ultimately, the Supreme Court.[1] In sum, Congress establishes the broad terms of the immigration contract, the president creates rules enforcing those terms, and the Supreme Court ensures that those terms are fair.

Understanding immigration policy as contract law and how the three branches of the federal government define the terms of that contract will help you better grasp how U.S. immigration law and policy have developed over time. What you will discover is that the U.S. Supreme Court has largely taken a backseat in the development of the law, allowing Congress and the president to shape immigration policy in ways that reinforce the idea that immigration law is essentially a contract and not a human rights policy, and that noncitizens are subject to restraints on their presence in the United States in ways that citizens are not.

At first blush, privileging U.S. citizens over foreigners might make intuitive sense. Any sovereign nation should be able to set the terms by which visitors to its shores enter and remain, on grounds inapplicable to those who are already full members of the polity. However, the history of congressional immigration policy is fraught with racial and ideological discrimination that has rarely been reviewed by the courts. The underlying idea here is that Congress, and by implication the U.S. citizens the lawmakers represent, are in the best position to set the terms of a noncitizen's sojourn in America; an unelected federal judiciary should not second-guess the will of the people as embodied in democratically enacted immigration policy.

While perhaps sound in principle, the historical legacy of Court deference to the legislature recently has had profound effects, as the United States seeks to determine what immigration policy would best suit a nation embroiled in a foreign war and whose citizens live in the shadow of September 11, 2001.

A Constitutional History of Racial and Ideological Exclusion in Deference to Congress

Much of the xenophobia that has gripped our post-9/11 world has its roots in the colonial period before the nation's founding. Whether escaping religious persecution or seeking better economic circumstances, many European arrivals to the New World brought their cultural baggage along with them, as the displaced Native Americans and imported African slaves soon found out. But the conquerors' prejudices also included nativist bigotry, for the Europeans often settled in ethnic enclaves, each group sticking to its own. It should come as no surprise, then, that Germantown, Pennsylvania, began as a village of Germans transplanted from the Old World in 1683.[2] The tendency to prefer things familiar and to demonize the foreign found its way into local anti-immigration policies that excluded certain religious groups and social classes. Certain colonial communities discouraged Quakers and Catholics, for example, from residing there due to these policies.

After independence in 1776, congressional forays into immigration policy were confined largely to naturalization measures, but otherwise, foreigners enjoyed an "open door" to the United States for about 100 years. This laissez-faire attitude toward immigration was born less of national largesse than of a lack of clarity as to who should have control over immigration—the thirteen states or the federal government. Then, as today, though the national government ultimately decided when and how a foreigner became a U.S. citizen, it was the states and local communities that felt the immediate impact of the noncitizen's migration. Because the fledgling nation was growing rapidly, the U.S. government was less concerned with limiting immigration than were the individual states, which viewed immigration control as but another manifestation of their reserved power. Thus, in contrast to states' wariness, the first federal legislation passed during this early period was the Facilitating Act of 1864, which sought to encourage immigration.

This tension between the federal and state governments over the power to limit foreign migration was perhaps an inevitable outgrowth of the new Constitution's lack of clarity. For instance, while Article I, Section 8, specifically grants power to Congress to "establish an [sic] uniform Rule of Naturalization" and to "regulate Commerce with foreign nations," nowhere in Article I or elsewhere does the federal government enjoy specific power to pass general immigration laws regulating the flow of foreigners from abroad. The word *migration* appears once in Article I, Section 9, but only in connection to the slave trade.

Because the founders understood that the federal government was one of limited power, the states continued to be most interested in regulating immigration, not only because they thought that this was a privilege reserved to them under the Constitution but also because, as a practical matter, they were most likely to feel the impact of a large immigrant influx. And so, it is perhaps unsurprising that founding father Benjamin Franklin, himself an immigrant, was concerned about the influx of German Catholics into his native Pennsylvania, just as many Californians and Arizonans today are concerned about the large migration of Latin Americans into the desert Southwest.

It was during the period between 1820 and 1880 that large numbers of German and Irish Catholics arrived in the United States to escape the European economic depression of the time, and in turn, some predominantly Protestant states passed laws in an attempt to stem the tide of Catholic migration. This nascent anti-immigrant movement proved unsuccessful at the federal level due to the aggregate political strength of the Irish and German migrants nationally.

Over time, this brewing conflict between federal and state power over immigration came to a head. The Supreme Court stepped in to resolve this dispute, ruling against the states and paving the way for Congress to begin crafting a uniform immigration policy for the nation. Following Supreme Court rulings in *The Passenger Cases* (1849)[3] and *Henderson v. Mayor of New York* (1875)[4] finding state immigration laws unconstitutional, Congress enacted the first general federal restrictions on immigration law in 1882, which included a fifty-cent head tax and exclusionary laws based on criminal and economic grounds. Although this first set of restrictions singled out no particular ethnic group for exclusion, the nativist sentiments that led to state laws against Catholic immigration found expression in a more particular piece of federal legislation that year.

It was in 1882 that Congress enacted immigration restrictions reminiscent of the states' recent anti-Catholic pronouncements when it passed the Chinese Exclusion Act. At first brought in to work on the westward expansion of the railroads, Chinese laborers fell into disfavor once they reached a critical mass and the work was completed. Unlike the religious and ideological divide that separated the Anglo-Saxon Protestants from the Irish and German Catholics, the growing distrust of the Chinese appeared more racial and cultural in origin. Because no large ethnic voting block protected the Chinese as it did the Catholics, Congress handily passed the Chinese Exclusion Act to prevent a further influx of these East Asian workers.

One such worker adversely affected by the law was Chae Chan Ping. A twelve-year resident of the United States, he had permission from the U.S. government to visit China, for which he received a certificate of return for presentation upon his reentry. At the border, however, U.S. officials revoked Chae Chan Ping's certificate and excluded him from reentering the United States under the Chinese Exclusion Act. Before the Supreme Court in *Chae Chan Ping v. United States* (1889),[5] Chae's lawyers argued that Congress could not unilaterally revoke his permit to briefly travel abroad. The Supreme Court flatly rejected that argument, holding that as a sovereign nation, the United States has the unilateral prerogative to make immigration policy as it sees fit, and noting that noncitizens enjoy no right to be in the United States. The Court then ruled that Congress had the power to exclude Chae because he was a member of a group, the Chinese, whom Congress had deemed undesirable. Its rhetoric regarding the inassimilable nature of the Chinese and the implication that they presented a threat to the United States even during peacetime evinces the xenophobia first evident in colonial restrictions on migration: "If, therefore, the government of the United States, through its legislative department, considers the presence of foreigners of a different race in this country, who will not assimilate with us, to be dangerous to its peace and security, their exclusion is not to be stayed because at the time there are no actual hostilities with the nation of which the foreigners are subjects."[6]

Four years later in *Fong Yue Ting v. United States* (1893),[7] the Court extended its holding in *Chae Chan Ping* by concluding that Congress had the power to deport or expel, also incident to its plenary power over immigration law. Perhaps even more disturbing than the rule the Court announced is that Fong's deportation resulted from his failure to come up with a "credible white witness" to testify to the length of his residence in the United States. Though Chinese nationals were ready to testify to Fong's continuous residence in the United States as the statute required, Fong was unable to secure such testimony from a white witness, perhaps owing to barriers created by culture and language, if not by racism. The Court found the "white witness" requirement to be neither irrational nor a denial of due process, deferring to Congress's judgment on the desirability of Chinese migration and the terms under which Chinese nationals must leave the United States. This privileging of the white witness in *Fong* mirrors the xenophobia of the inassimilable Chinese in *Chae*.

While good reasons support the Court's deferral to Congress in both *Chae Chan Ping* and *Fong Yue Ting*, these reasons pale in comparison to the racism afoot in both opinions. On the one hand, it is true that the structure and functions of the Constitution argue that Congress, and not the Court, should be in charge of formulating immigration law and policy because it is the lawmaking body of the federal government. This exclusive power of Congress over immigration law came to be known as the "plenary power doctrine": as the legislative organ of the federal government, Congress has the sole right to determine what laws govern the entry and exclusion of those persons who are not citizens of the United States.

On the other hand, the very structure of the Constitution requires that the Court stand vigilant in making sure that Congress does not abuse its plenary power and that its immigration policies are fundamentally fair to noncitizens. Put another way, the Court has the responsibility of reviewing legislative action when it appears that the terms of Congress's contract with the noncitizen violate a central constitutional truth. In a case decided just a few years before *Chae* and *Fong*, the Court held in *Yick Wo v. Hopkins* (1886)[8] that San Francisco could not discriminate against Chinese nationals by denying them permits to operate laundries solely on the basis of their race. Invoking the Constitution's equal protection clause, the Court concluded that a local government could not make race a factor in determining how to enforce the terms of a municipal ordinance. To do so would treat Chinese noncitizens and others unequally under a law that was designed not to limit immigration to the United States but to regulate the safety of laundries in San Francisco.

In contrast to *Yick Wo*, the Court in both *Chae* and *Fong* failed to place a check on Congress's power over immigration law by allowing it to make race and national origin factors in determining whether these foreign workers could remain in the United States. In *Chae*, it was the plaintiff's foreignness alone that made it permissible for Congress to renege on its promise to readmit him into the country, whereas in *Fong* it was the Chinese man's failure to find a white witness that led to his deportation.

The secret to reconciling these seemingly disparate cases—*Yick Wo* favoring the noncitizen versus *Chae* and *Fong* favoring the government—lies in understanding the separate roles the federal and state governments play with regard to immigration policy. As we saw earlier, the Court in the late nineteenth century struck down state immigration laws, and once Congress started enacting its own restrictive migration policies, the Court affirmatively approved these. This guidance by the Court made clear that while both the state and federal legislatures may want to restrict immigration, the Constitution has given that power to Congress, not the states. Even though San Francisco's laundry ordinance in *Yick Wo* did not purport to restrict immigration, observers saw it as an attempt to discriminate against Chinese nationals, something that the city, as a state municipality, could not do. Such laws that indirectly seek to influence immigration by directly targeting noncitizens have come to be known as "alienage law," whether passed by the state, local, or federal government. In contrast, *Chae* and *Fong* make clear that Congress can directly set the terms of a noncitizen's immigration contract on virtually any grounds, even on racial grounds the Court would not condone at the municipal level in *Yick Wo*.

After the creation of the plenary power doctrine through *Chae Chan Ping* and its progeny, Congress took full advantage of this newfound strength by passing many laws restricting immigration, ranging from the exclusion of the "pauper" and the polygamist to the expulsion of the Asian and the "anarchist." Notable among these was the National Origins Quota system established in 1924, which pegged permissible immigration to 2 percent of the number of persons from that country as reflected in the census. While facially neutral, the quota operated as a bar to Asian migration, following on the heels of the Chinese Exclusion Act of 1882 and the 1917 establishment of an "Asiatic barred zone."

The 1950s saw another period of nativistic sentiment, this time highlighting ideology rather than race as a legitimate ground for discriminating against noncitizens. Following World War II and the advent of the Cold War, Congress and the president turned to a stricter enforcement of ideological bases for excluding and deporting noncitizens, supported in their efforts by the Supreme Court. Just as it did in *Chae* and *Fong*, the Court would not stand in the way of the federal legislature's and executive's decisions to privilege democracy over communism, despite the negative impact upon longtime residents of the United States.

In *Shaughnessy v. United States ex rel. Mezei* (1953),[9] for instance, the Court upheld the four-year detention of Ignatz Mezei on Ellis Island following his return from visiting his dying mother in Romania. Because immigration officials were concerned that Mezei, a twenty-five-year noncitizen resident of the United States, had spent nineteen months "behind the Iron Curtain,"[10] the Court deferred to Congress's and the executive's judgment that his detention without charge was a national security concern. It did so without specific proof of why Mezei was a threat to the nation; the Court simply accepted the political branches' representations that he was one. As in the Chinese Exclusion Act cases, the Court believed its proper role was to defer to the reasoned judgment of the other two federal branches, even without specific proof that the individual noncitizens—all longtime guests of the nation—had violated the terms of their stay in the United States.

In addition to the more stringent emphasis on ideological concerns, Congress and the executive continued their promulgation and enforcement of racially discriminatory immigration policies, though this time a bit more subtly. In 1952, Congress passed the McCarran-Walter Act,[11] a comprehensive immigration bill that forms the framework of modern U.S. immigration law today, but included within it a more restrictive version of the National Origins Quota system and established a new special racial quota for Asians. The U.S. Attorney General also repatriated 1.3 million Mexicans (and, it turns out, Mexican Americans) during the infamous "Operation Wetback," designed to combat undocumented migration.

Some commentators have argued that the historical discrimination on race and ideological grounds merely mirrored the domestic discrimination citizens suffered as well.[12] Minority citizens—whether on account of race, gender, or sexual orientation—received few protections from the U.S. government; it should be no surprise, then, that noncitizens in the same groups also suffered accordingly. If true, it may be argued that the plenary power doctrine should be divorced from its racist origins and possesses independent value: the doctrine properly places immigration law within the political realm, outside the purview of unelected federal judges. As the political climate changes, the laws change through amended legislation, not by judicial fiat. Indeed, several congressional initiatives have corrected the sins of the past, including the 1965 abolition of the National Origins Quota system (which has led to a large influx of Asian immigration) and the passing of the Refugee Act of 1980 (the beneficiaries of which have been largely from communist regimes).

But the near-total deference afforded the political branches through the plenary power doctrine may come at a high price to human rights. This question of how to balance the role of the federal courts as a check against the executive and the legislature is of particular concern to many noncitizens post-9/11. Moreover, as de facto "first responders," what role do states and local governments play in a regime in which the Constitution confers immigration power exclusively upon the federal government?

Two Limits on Federal and State Power over Noncitizens

While the Court has consistently affirmed the original plenary power doctrine born of the Chinese Exclusion Act cases, it has also developed two other themes in an attempt to carve out a role for itself and the states in the immigration policy debate. First, the Court recognizes it has the authority to tell Congress when it has gone too far in imposing conditions upon the noncitizen that violate his or her basic rights as an individual. It has done so subtly, either by requiring Congress and the executive to provide for constitutional due process safeguards or by reading statutes and regulations broadly to protect noncitizens from arbitrary treatment. Second, the Court has held that states have only a limited role in regulating the activity of noncitizens under so-called alienage law. While states are free to place limits on the activities of noncitizens that go to the heart of political governance, they may not enact legislation that discriminates against noncitizens in their eligibility for public benefits as an alternative to directly preventing them from settling into their state.

Constitutional and Statutory Limits on the Federal Government
Constitutional Limits via the Due Process Clause
Landon v. Plasencia (1982)[13] is one prominent example of the Court requiring the then Immigration and Naturalization Service (INS) to provide a noncitizen with a hearing in accord with the Constitution's due process clause. Salvadoran national Maria Plasencia, a lawful permanent resident for ten years, had left the United States for a brief two-day visit to Mexico. Upon her reentry, federal authorities charged her with smuggling undocumented persons into the U.S. knowingly and "for gain." An immigration judge summarily excluded Plasencia from entry after an expedited hearing at which she would ordinarily have been entitled to free legal counsel under then-existing rules. Because of her limited English, however, she had unknowingly waived her right to such assistance.[14] The "for gain" portion of the charge also bespeaks injustice and careless prosecuting. While the evidence suggested that she provided a ride to undocumented individuals whom she met in Tijuana, it is unclear whether Plasencia knew that they were undocumented and even less clear whether she had received any money for transporting them. Nonetheless, the immigration judge found her excludable, which

would have required her separation from her U.S. citizen husband and children. The Supreme Court vacated the immigration judge's order, finding that Plasencia had not been given due process in light of her substantial connections to the United States: "Plasencia's interest here is, without question, a weighty one. She stands to lose the right 'to stay and live and work in this land of freedom.' Further, she may lose the right to rejoin her immediate family, a right that ranks high among the interests of the individual."[15]

In reviewing "alienage law"—the law affecting noncitizens in the U.S. aside and apart from the entry and exit rules of immigration law—courts subject federal legislation to a "rational basis" test that has only occasionally resulted in invalidating discriminatory legislation. Under such review, the Court will generally defer to the government's reasons for enacting legislation if these appear reasonable. However, if the Court believes that the federal government has unfairly singled out noncitizens for unfavorable treatment, it will strike down legislation even under the deferential rational basis standard.

A good example of a deferential application of rational basis review appears in *Mathews v. Diaz* (1976).[16] Lawful permanent residents (LPRs)—so-called green card holders—had challenged federal Medicare rules that only allowed for supplemental insurance benefits to those who had been in the country for at least five years. Applying a deferential rational basis review, the Court held that it was reasonable for Congress to condition receipt of these federal benefits on the length of an LPR's stay, noting that those who had been in the United States longer may have stronger ties to the nation.

In contrast, *Hampton v. Mow Sun Wong* (1976)[17] stands as an example of when rational basis review may be used to strike down laws that irrationally discriminate against noncitizens. LPRs challenged U.S. Civil Service Commission regulations excluding all noncitizens from occupying federal civil service jobs, limiting such occupations to U.S. citizens and natives of American Samoa. Applying what appeared to be a more stringent version of the rational basis test than in *Mathews*, the Court ruled that the government's desire for administrative convenience did not outweigh lawful noncitizens' rights to be considered equally for such jobs as U.S. citizens.

Statutory Limits Through Interpretations Favorable to Noncitizens
Aside from directly invoking procedural due process protections as in *Landon* or employing a more stringent rational basis review as in

Hampton, the Court has also interpreted immigration statutes broadly to protect noncitizens from government overreaching. In *Zadvydas v. Davis* (2001),[18] the Court ruled that authorities could not hold a lawful permanent resident indefinitely pending the government's efforts to deport him. Following a finding that Zadvydas was deportable for having committed certain crimes, the government had sought to remove him but could find no country willing to accept him; it therefore argued that it could detain Zadvydas indefinitely until it could effect his deportation, citing the 1953 *Mezei* case as precedent.[19] The government reasoned that if it could hold Mezei, a returning lawful permanent resident, indefinitely at Ellis Island on national security grounds, then it could also hold Zadvydas because his criminal conduct vitiated his right to remain in the United States. The Court rejected this argument, finding that Congress intended to place a limit of reasonableness on a deportee's length of detention pending deportation. Concerned that a statute authorizing the indefinite detention of noncitizens would raise serious due process problems, the Court required the government to deport individuals within six months.

In 2005 the Court extended the holding of *Zadvydas* regarding deportable noncitizens to excludable noncitizens as well, thereby effectively limiting *Mezei*'s reach. *Clark v. Martinez* (2005)[20] had its origins in the Mariel boatlift twenty-five years earlier. Embarking from the port of Mariel, approximately 125,000 Cubans arrived in the United States as refugees in 1980; most of these "Marielitos" had relatives in the United States whom they rejoined, eventually becoming lawful permanent residents. The INS had identified 2,746 individuals as being risks to public safety, however, because they either had committed serious crimes or had suffered from severe mental illnesses that rendered them dangerous to others. Under immigration law, it was as if these persons had never arrived: like Chae Chan Ping and Mezei before them, these 2,746 Cubans would not be permitted to legally and formally enter the United States because of the danger they posed to the public—in technical parlance, they were "inadmissible." Cuba would not accept them back, but because of the threat they posed to safety, the INS was also unwilling to release them from detention, opting instead to temporarily "parole" them pending their removal. Unfortunately, many of those released committed crimes, prompting the government to re-detain them.

At issue in *Clark v. Martinez* was whether *Mezei* allowed the government to indefinitely detain these otherwise excludable Cubans or whether the logic of *Zadvydas* placed reasonable limits on the government's detention power. The Court chose to extend *Zadvydas* to cover the inadmissible Cubans, holding that it was Congress's presumptive intent that all noncitizens regardless of status—whether deportable or inadmissible—should not be detained for more than six months pending their removal. Undergirding this opinion was the Fifth Amendment's due process clause, which the Court in both *Clark* and *Zadvydas* saw as the basis for reading Congress's intent in favor of the noncitizens, thereby limiting the government's power over them.

Constitutional Limits on the States

In contrast to the general deference accorded Congress in formulating policies affecting noncitizens both within and outside the immigration rules, the Court has more strictly scrutinized state laws as it did in *Yick Wo*, holding that states have only a limited role in regulating the activity of noncitizens under alienage law. While states are free to place limits on the activities of noncitizens that directly impinge on the democratic process, they may not enact legislation that discriminates against noncitizens in their eligibility for state public benefits as a means to discourage them from residing in-state.

Unlike the deferential rational basis test employed by the Court to review federal alienage law in *Mathews* and *Hampton*, *Graham v. Richardson* (1971)[21] applied a more searching "strict scrutiny" test to root out invidious state discrimination against noncitizens. In *Graham*, the Court invalidated state welfare laws that contained citizenship and durational residency requirements that unfairly discriminated against noncitizens. The main difference between *Graham* (a state benefits law case) and *Mathews* (a federal benefits case) appears to be the degree to which the Court was willing to substitute its judgment for the legislature's. Whereas in *Graham* the Court was willing to second-guess the legislature, in *Mathews* it wasn't. Hence, it is unsurprising that in *Sugarman v. Dougall* (1973),[22] the Court struck down an anti-noncitizen state civil service rule similar to the federal one in Hampton.

The reason for the difference in the Court's treatment of the two sets of law stems from its view of the proper role of the federal and state governments vis-à-vis noncitizens. Because Congress enjoys plenary power over immigration policy, it makes sense that Congress should also enjoy some leeway in other federal laws it passes that affect noncitizens during their visit. States, in contrast, have no power to grant U.S. citizenship under the Constitution, nor do they have a say in who gets to enter and who has to leave. Although contested at our nation's founding, it is now commonly understood that immigration law is a federal, not state, matter; if a state decides that it wants to indirectly influence a noncitizen's residential choices by passing restrictive state laws, the Court will examine those with a keen eye to ensure that some higher, more important governmental objective is present than simply the desire to conserve resources for U.S. citizens and LPRs first. Given that governments often use national origin as a proxy for racial discrimination (think of both the Japanese internment during World War II and the post-9/11 profiling of Muslims and Arabs), the Court holds states more accountable than the federal government for laws adversely affecting their noncitizen populations. The stricter scrutiny applied to state action has led to the invalidation of a host of laws, from citizenship limitations on the ability to practice law[23] to the ineligibility for financial aid for college based on alienage.[24]

The Court has even protected undocumented immigrant children from state discrimination, applying a slightly less severe standard than strict scrutiny. In *Plyler v. Doe* (1982)[25] the Court struck down a Texas law that denied free public education to elementary and secondary school children of undocumented immigrants. Writing for a 5-to-4 majority, Justice Brennan applied what appeared to be an intermediate level of scrutiny, reasoning that because the children innocently accompanied their parents into this country, denying them the right to an education would impose a grave disability and create a permanent underclass of uneducated children.

Despite the Court's preference for strict review, in one class of cases the Court has deferred to state alienage laws, sometimes called the "public function" exception.[26] In *Ambach v. Norwick* (1979) the Court refused to apply strict scrutiny to state alienage classifications "that exclude [noncitizens] from positions intimately related to the process of democratic self-government."[27] Hence, in *Foley v. Connelie* (1978)[28] the Court upheld a New York state law limiting police officer jobs to U.S. citizens only, reasoning that police are vested with a great deal of discretionary power to maintain law and order—power that, in the state's view, should not be given to noncitizens over citizens.

Predictions for the Future: A Greater Enforcement Role for States as Congress Continues to Define the Nation's Immigration Contract?

If we have learned one thing from this brief tour of the nature and history of U.S. immigration law and policy, it is that Congress is the main governmental entity responsible for changes in America's contract with noncitizens. While that law may at times appear to be protective of human rights and dignity (in its refugee and amnesty laws, for instance) and at other times draconian and uncaring (in its denial of judicial review or its expedited deportation procedures), one should appreciate it for what it is: a list of rules governing the conditions under which noncitizens may enter and must leave the United States. It is more like a contract than a human rights document, and in the United States, Congress has the near-exclusive power to define the terms of that contract.

To see this, we need only review one recent Supreme Court pronouncement on the rights of noncitizens under federal immigration law and policy, a decision that reflects the judiciary's continued deference to congressional plenary power. As noted in *Fernandez-Vargas v. Gonzales* (2006),[29] Mexican national Humberto Fernandez-Vargas first entered the United States lawfully in the 1970s but was ordered deported for immigration violations several times. His final reentry occurred in 1982, and for approximately twenty years thereafter, he remained undetected. His life, however, had taken a turn for the better: he started his own trucking business in Utah, bore a U.S. citizen son, and in 1999 married the son's mother, his longtime girlfriend, who is also a U.S. citizen. When his wife petitioned for his adjustment to lawful immigrant status in 2001, the federal government reinstated his 1981 deportation order, denied his application for status adjustment, and eventually deported him to Mexico.

The issue before the Supreme Court was whether the government acted lawfully in resurrecting his now twenty-year-old deportation order pursuant to a federal law that had not been enacted until many years after Fernandez-Vargas had returned to the United States and become a productive member of the community. In an 8-to-1 decision, the Supreme Court interpreted the 1996 law, the Illegal Immigration Reform and Immigrant Responsibility Act (IIRAIRA), in the government's favor, upholding the government's reinstatement of the deportation order and Fernandez-Vargas's subsequent removal to Mexico. One might argue that Fernandez-Vargas should not have benefited from his ability to evade the authorities for twenty years; yet, one can easily imagine a judge weighing the equities in this case of a reformed man whose deportation would have devastating consequences for his U.S. citizen child and spouse.

Fernandez-Vargas v. Gonzales stands as but one recent example in a string of Supreme Court cases that underscore the plenary power of Congress over immigration matters and lends support to the idea that immigration law is more like contract law than human rights law. Fernandez-Vargas violated the terms of his contract with the United States and was held responsible for his breach; a human rights version of immigration law might have insisted on an impartial arbiter's review of the government's interest in maintaining order balanced against the noncitizen's reformation.

We have also learned that states have less of a role to play in enforcing or enacting immigration law than does the federal government, although we are likely to see more state and local governments seek ways to address immigration-related issues. The reality is that state and local authorities have exhibited growing frustration with the federal government's response to immigration issues, especially with respect to the undocumented.

With an estimated 12 million and counting, undocumented immigrants have a significant impact in a handful of states and localities, and some argue that among the poor and lower classes, in terms of competition for jobs, many have become disillusioned by the perennial underfunding of immigration initiatives and the perceived lax federal approach to immigration enforcement. Yet, others maintain that immigration confers a net economic benefit to Americans and that undocumented immigrants form the backbone of a significant number of industries, from farming to construction to textiles; thus, even if feasible, the mass deportation of all undocumented persons would severely damage these businesses and the national economy.[30]

It will be interesting to see whether state and local governments will gain a greater ability to enforce immigration laws in the future.[31]

Indeed, the federal government has already created memoranda of understanding with several state and local police forces in an effort to gain their assistance in apprehending immigration violators.[32] As a state's role in immigration enforcement expands, and as the federal government's role correspondingly wanes, scholars and pundits alike will pay close attention to the Supreme Court's response to this paradigm shift. Whether the Court will hold on to its traditional skepticism of state actions against noncitizens or begin to defer to such initiatives as emanating from valid congressional mandates, only time will tell.

Now that you understand the basic history of immigration policy-making and the respective roles of the state and federal governments in its formulation, let us turn in Chapter 2 to the essential rules that govern noncitizens' entry into and departure from the United States. We will try to understand the reasons why a noncitizen may be allowed to enter—is it to unite families, facilitate labor transfer, or provide sanctuary?—as well as why he or she may be required to leave.

Notes

1. A similar case involving Haitian refugees' challenge to the president's "interdiction" policy was decided by the Supreme Court in *Sale v. Haitian Centers Council, Inc.*, 509 U.S. 155 (1993).

2. Roger Daniels, *Coming to America: A History of Immigration and Ethnicity in American Life*, 1st ed. (New York: HarperCollins, 1990), 19 ("Whereas one generalizes about migration from Europe, from England, and from Italy going to the New World, to the American Colonies, and to the cities of the northeastern United States, the fact of the matter is that migration often follows more precise patterns, often from a particular region, city, or village in the sending country to specific regions, cities, or even specific city blocks in the receiving nation"). For instance, the first major German migration to the American colonies, in 1683, resulted because villagers from Krefeld, Germany, decided to move en masse to establish what is now Germantown, Pennsylvania.

3. 48 U.S. 283 (1849).

4. 92 U.S. 259 (1875).

5. 130 U.S. 581 (1889). Hiroshi Motomura believes *Chae Chan Ping* supports the idea that our immigration policy operates like contract law. See Hiroshi Motomura, *Americans in Waiting: The Lost Story of Immigration and Citizenship in the United States* (New York: Oxford University Press,

2006), 15 ("Chae Chan Ping's case is a prime example of the view of immigration that I am calling immigration as contract").

6. Ibid., 606.

7. 149 U.S. 698 (1893).

8. 118 U.S. 356 (1886). Jack Chin argues that *Yick Wo* was actually not too remarkable as an equal protection case but was rather a property rights case consistent with existing precedent. Specifically, he claims that it narrowly stands for the proposition that treaty obligations to the Chinese trumped the state's ability to regulate against them. See Gabriel J. Chin, *Unexplainable on Grounds of Race: Doubts About* Yick Wo, available at http://papers.ssrn.com/sol3/papers.cfm?abstract_id=1075563 (last visited on Jan. 29, 2008).

9. 345 U.S. 206 (1953).

10. Ibid., 214.

11. The annotations to the original statute read, "The Immigration and Nationality Act, referred to in subsec. (a)(1), is Act June 27, 1952, c. 477, 66 Stat. 163, as amended, which is classified principally to chapter 12 of this title [8 U.S.C.A. 1101 et seq.], and is also known as the INA, the McCarran Act, and the McCarran-Walter Act."

12. See, e.g., Kevin R. Johnson, *The "Huddled Masses Myth": Immigration and Civil Rights* (Philadelphia: Temple University Press, 2003); and Gabriel J. Chin, "Is There a Plenary Power Doctrine? A Tentative Apology and Prediction for Our Strange but Unexceptional Constitutional Immigration Law," 14 *Georgetown Immigration Law Journal* 257 (2000).

13. 459 U.S. 21 (1982).

14. Ibid., 35. These facts are described more fully in Kevin Johnson's description of the case in the anthology *Immigration Law Stories*, edited by Peter H. Schuck and David A. Martin (New York: Foundation Press, 2005).

15. 459 U.S. 34.

16. 426 U.S. 67 (1976).

17. 426 U.S. 88 (1976).

18. 533 U.S. 678 (2001).

19. This consolidated case also involved a second criminal noncitizen, Ma, whom no other country would accept.

20. 543 U.S. 371 (2005).

21. 403 U.S. 365 (1971).

22. 413 U.S. 634 (1973).

23. *In re Griffiths*, 413 U.S. 717 (1973).

24. *Nyquist v. Mauclet*, 432 U.S. 1 (1977).

25. 457 U.S. 202 (1982).

26. See, e.g., Michael Scaperlanda, "Partial Membership: Aliens and the Constitutional Community," 81 *Iowa Law Review* 707, 736 (1996) (describing the "public function" exception).

27. 441 U.S. 68, 75 (1979).

28. 435 U.S. 291 (1978).

29. 548 U.S. 30 (2006).

30. See, e.g., June 19, 2006, Open Letter to President Bush on Immigration from 500+ Economists and Social Scientists, available at http://www .independent.org/newsroom/article.asp?id=1727 (last visited on Mar. 13, 2008) (arguing net economic benefit to U.S. from immigration).

31. For a collection of thoughtful essays on this issue, see the New York University Annual Survey of American Law 2002 Symposium, "Migration Regulation Goes Local: The Role of States in U.S. Immigration Policy," especially Mike Wishnie's introduction to the symposium on p. 58.

32. Jeff Sessions and Cynthia Hayden, "The Growing Role for State and Local Law Enforcement in the Realm of Immigration Law," 16 *Stanford Law and Policy Review* 323, 345 (2005).

2

Immigration Law Basics

As we learned in Chapter 1, two sets of laws govern noncitizens in the United States: immigration law and alienage law. The first encompasses only the rules under which noncitizens are allowed to enter and must leave the United States, while the second focuses on the substantive rights and responsibilities of noncitizens under other federal, state, and local laws. For example, making sure that one has a valid visa is an immigration law requirement; whether a noncitizen is eligible to receive a state driver's license is part of alienage law. For some, discriminating against noncitizens outside immigration law serves the same purpose as deportation: it is an effort to remove noncitizens by limiting their access to certain benefits.

This chapter devotes its attention to the basics of immigration law. Accordingly, the focus will be on the rules governing *admission* (when a noncitizen may enter and under what status) and *removal* (when a noncitizen must leave). My goal is to give you a bird's-eye view of basic immigration law so that when you seek help for a specific problem (be it filling out visa petition forms or avoiding deportation), you will be better equipped to determine whether you may be able to solve the problem yourself or require the assistance of qualified counsel. Here's a fair rule of thumb: while it may be possible to complete many nonimmigrant and immigrant documents without hiring a lawyer when one seeks to enter the United States for the first time, it would be foolish to go without one when faced with deportation, especially if one has lived in the United States for many years and developed significant ties to this country.

We learned in Chapter 1 that Congress has the power to set immigration rules. It did so in the Immigration and Nationality Act (INA, a confusing labyrinth even to seasoned lawyers).[1] This chapter will highlight the basics of the INA's admission and removal rules.

Admission to the United States

Every noncitizen who wishes to enter the United States must abide by the INA's admission rules, which divide all noncitizens into two groups: immigrants and nonimmigrants. Immigrants, or "lawful permanent residents" (LPRs), intend to make the United States their home; as their designation suggests, they want to reside permanently in the United States. Nonimmigrants, in comparison, intend only to stay in the United States for a brief time period and a specific purpose; they do not want to abandon their home residence. Each group has its own application process and receives its own specific visa, or entry document. Aside from these general categories, the immigration code contains specific provisions that benefit noncitizens from certain nations. For instance, in 2005 Congress created a nonimmigrant visa specifically to benefit Australian nationals in certain specialty occupations, pursuant to the U.S.-Australia Free Trade Agreement.[2] I will discuss a few of the more important country-specific rules throughout this discussion. My goal is to give you sufficient information to understand the differences within and between the various immigrant and nonimmigrant categories, leaving discussion of the major procedural rules to Chapter 3.

Immigrants (U.S. Citizens-to-Be)

Immigrants or LPRs want to make the United States their home. These so-called green card holders (the LPR cards used to be green in color) intend to abandon their residence in their home country and live permanently in the United States. Contrary to what most people think, a noncitizen can immigrate to the United States in only *four* ways: (1) through a valid family relationship; (2) by obtaining gainful employment; (3) by being a refugee or asylee; or (4) by winning the diversity visa lottery. Specific, narrow grounds set out when one may immigrate, and as will be discussed in a separate section, each category has its own specific rules that further lessen the chances one has to immigrate. For example, a U.S. citizen may not file a petition for his foreign grandchildren to immigrate, although he may petition for his foreign children.

One rule that benefits family members of immigrants concerns *derivative beneficiaries,* which are the spouses and unmarried children of beneficiaries of an immigrant visa petition. Hence, if a U.S. citizen were to petition his brother under the category for siblings of U.S. citizens, his brother's wife would be able to accompany him as a derivative beneficiary. She would receive the same visa status as the brother.[3]

To guide our discussion, I have outlined the different immigrant classifications in Figure 2.1.

Family Relationships
U.S. citizens or LPRs may petition to have certain family relatives from abroad immigrate to live with them in the United States. The goal is to help promote family unity. If it is granted, the foreign beneficiaries receive what may be termed *family-sponsored visas.*

These family-sponsored visas fall into two types: those not subject to numerical quotas, and those that are. The quotas are meant to control the number of noncitizens who may enter the United States. Because the number of applicants far exceeds the number of visas available each year, the backlogs can be great. These processing backlogs are reported monthly in the State Department's *Visa Bulletin,* which is available at http://travel.state.gov/visa/frvi/bulletin/bulletin_1360.html. When reading the bulletin, you will note that certain countries—mainland China, Mexico, India, and the Philippines—have their own separate waiting times; this is because the number of applications from these four nations is particularly large. Let's return to our example of the resident petitioning his brother from the Philippines. If he filed an immigrant petition on his brother's behalf today, it would take over twenty years before his visa would be available because the government is processing visas in this category from the 1980s!

To avoid delay, it is advantageous to see if the relative you want to petition can qualify as an immigrant not subject to a quota, also known as an "immediate relative."[4] A U.S. citizen may petition a noncitizen as an immediate relative if the beneficiary is a spouse,[5] child (i.e., an unmarried son or daughter under twenty-one years of age, including certain adopted and stepchildren),[6] or parent[7] of that citizen. Congress has established no quotas for these relatives because

Figure 2.1 Immigrants (U.S. Citizens-to-Be)

Family Relationships
- Not Subject to Quotas
  - Immediate Relatives of U.S. Citizen
    (spouse, child, or parent of U.S. citizen)
- Subject to Quotas
  - First Preference
    (unmarried sons and daughters of U.S. citizens who are at least 21 years old)
  - Second Preference
    (spouse, children, and unmarried sons and daughters of LPRs)
  - Third Preference
    (married sons and daughters of U.S. citizens)
  - Fourth Preference
    (siblings of U.S. citizens)

Employment Relationships
- First Preference/ Priority Workers
  - Extraordinary Ability in the Sciences, Arts, Education, Business, or Athletics
  - Outstanding Professors and Researchers
  - Certain Multinational Executives and Managers
- Second Preference
  - Professionals with Advanced Degrees and Exceptional Ability in the Sciences, Arts, or Business
- Third Preference
  - Professionals
  - Skilled Workers
  - Other Workers
- Fourth Preference
  - Special Immigrants
- Fifth Preference
  - Employer-Investors

Refugees and Asylees

Diversity Visa Lottery Winners

it has determined that their relationships to the petitioning citizen are the most important to process expeditiously. Although no quotas affect this group, the number of immediate relatives who immigrate decreases the annual quota of visas available for other family-sponsored categories in subsequent years.

Unlike immediate relatives, the four remaining immigrant categories are all subject to quotas that differ depending on category and country of origin. They are:

First preference—Unmarried sons and daughters of U.S. citizens (note that individuals in this category are at least twenty-one years old, which would distinguish them from immediate relative "children");

Second preference—Spouse, children, and unmarried sons and daughters of LPRs (lawful permanent residents);

Third preference—Married sons and daughters of U.S. citizens; and

Fourth preference—Siblings of U.S. citizens.

Two observations are worth pointing out. First, note that many common, generally recognized family statuses do not qualify a person to receive immigration benefits, including grandparents, uncles and aunts, nieces and nephews, and cousins. It does not matter that a U.S. citizen may enjoy a closer relationship to her foreign aunt than to her mother—under immigration law, she may petition only her mother, not her aunt. And second, of the five family-sponsored immigrant categories, only one—the second preference category—covers relatives of LPRs; the rest benefit relatives of U.S. citizens only. An LPR who has lived in the U.S. for twenty years will thus have fewer opportunities to sponsor relatives abroad than a U.S. citizen who has lived here for only five years; this creates an incentive for LPRs to naturalize and become U.S. citizens, which many do despite having to put up with seemingly interminable backlogs and delays.

It is fair to say, therefore, that while family unity is an important value, Congress has specified which relationships are most valuable and which petitioners should be given preference. It is clear that nuclear family members (i.e., spouses and children, along with older parents) are most preferred and that U.S. citizens receive priority over LPRs.

Employment Relationships

Like the family-sponsored visas, employment-based visas also fall into preference categories according to work and skills.[8] Five employment-based visa categories come with different qualifications and requirements. Because the employment categories use specific language that is less familiar and more technical than the family-based ones (i.e., most everyone understands the term *parent* but perhaps not *priority worker*), I include some specific examples of individuals who may or may not qualify for these visas.

First Preference. "Priority workers"[9] fit into one of three categories: (1) persons of "extraordinary ability" in the sciences, arts, education, business, or athletics; (2) outstanding professors and researchers; and (3) certain multinational executives and managers. Immigration scholar Steve Legomsky refers to all of these workers as "superstars": individuals who have reached the highest levels of their profession[10] and whose designation as priority workers reflects Congress's decision that they should be able to immigrate to the U.S. easily.

Those in the first group ("extraordinary ability") must evince "a level of expertise indicating that [they are] one of that small percentage who have risen to the very top of the field of endeavor."[11] These individuals are so exceptional that they need not demonstrate they have a job in the United States, but instead may file for immigrant status on their own. Immigration expert Allan Wernick relates the fictional stories of Ying Shu and Chudi as examples of persons who fall into this elite group.[12] Ying Shu is one of the world's leading Chinese zither players; although not well-known in the United States, she is a household name within China and in Chinese-speaking communities throughout the world, having released several best-selling albums and played to packed theaters in New York and San Francisco. Her immigration petition for LPR status contained supporting documentation of her achievements, including letters from experts on Chinese music, many of her album covers, articles about her in U.S. and Chinese periodicals, and a letter from her agent attesting to her performance schedule for the coming year.

Chudi came to the United States on a temporary work visa (H-1B) as a reporter for the *Los Angeles Gazette,* commonly regarded as one of the outstanding news dailies in the country, having worked previously for Nigeria's leading newspaper. Chudi was soon promoted to chief international reporter and received many national and international reporting awards; his work appeared in many national and international publications. When he submitted his immigrant petition, his supporting documentation included letters from journalists, professors, and editors of three leading U.S. newsmagazines attesting to Chudi's status as a leading writer on international events.

Scholars who qualify to be in the second group are deemed "outstanding" because they enjoy international recognition in their field, demonstrated by their published works, awards, or other indicia.[13] Unlike those in the first group, these individuals may not self-petition but instead must be sponsored by their employers. Hence, expert Wernick opines, a researcher with many years of experience and publications in internationally recognized journals would likely qualify for this status, while an outstanding classroom teacher who has published in popular periodicals only would likely not.

Businesspersons in the third group must have served in managerial capacities at foreign firms that have an American affiliate for at least one of the previous three years. The purpose of this visa is to facilitate the transfer of international workers. As an example, consider the fictional case of Katherine:[14] she works for a British bank that has a New York office. She arrived in New York on a temporary international transferee visa (L-1) and was assigned to manage the international investment division. In that capacity, she reported directly to the president of the bank's New York operations and supervised many employees, including investment advisors, financial analysts, and secretaries. After two years in New York, she asked her home office to help her immigrate; the president of the New York branch filed a first-preference employment-based petition on her behalf, and she received LPR status.

It perhaps goes without saying that although the United States allocates a substantial number of visas for this first preference category, very few immigrants qualify for them; hence, unlike in the family-based categories, the number of available visas exceeds that of qualified immigrants.

Second Preference. These are professionals with "advanced degrees" or persons of "exceptional ability" in the sciences, arts, or business. To correct differences in language between the first and second preference categories, the term *arts* includes athletes and entertainers.[15] "Advanced degrees" are academic or professional degrees beyond the bachelor's. A bachelor's degree plus five years of progressive work experience may substitute for a master's degree, unless the immigrant's field typically requires a doctorate.[16] "Exceptional ability" is a shade below the first preference's "extraordinary ability"; it refers to a degree of expertise significantly above that of those ordinarily in the field. Possessing a professional degree or license is insufficient evidence, by itself, of exceptional ability.[17] Thus, a nationally recognized concert musician would likely qualify as exceptional, but an average musician who makes a living from playing in bars would not.[18]

Both the "advanced degree" and "exceptional ability" prongs of this category require a U.S. employer to file a petition on the immigrant's behalf as well as an application for labor certification before the U.S. Department of Labor. This labor certification attests that no lawful U.S. workers—that is, U.S. citizens and LPRs, asylees, and refugees—are ready, willing, and able to fill the job offered. While some mistakenly believe that an immigrant must possess unique qualifications to obtain labor certification, employers may often meet this requirement by demonstrating, for example, that the immigrant has more years of experience than other U.S. workers.[19] It is important to keep in mind, however, that an immigrant must receive both labor certification and a valid employment-based visa to enter the United States. One without the other is insufficient.

One notable exception to the labor certification requirement is the "national interest" waiver, so called because the United States decides it is in the best interests of the nation that the immigrant be allowed to work here. Thus, foreign physicians who agree to work in underserved communities for at least five years are entitled to these waivers upon the recommendation of a federal or state agency that their work will be in the public interest.[20] For instance, McAllen, Texas, and other cities along the U.S.-Mexican border have long employed foreign medical graduates willing to provide their services because these are areas U.S. workers traditionally underserve.

Third Preference. Three subcategories comprise the third-preference group: (1) "professionals," (2) "skilled workers," and (3) "other workers." Also falling in the second preference category, "professionals" include architects, engineers, lawyers, physicians, surgeons, and teachers,[21] as well as those in other occupations that require at least a bachelor's degree.[22] "Skilled workers" are individuals who are capable of performing a job that requires at least two years of education, training, or experience.[23] Finally, "other workers" are unskilled[24] laborers whose jobs require less than two years of training or experience.[25] Significantly, only 10,000 of the 40,000 annual visas allocated to the third preference category are allotted for unskilled laborers, leading to a long wait list of many years.[26]

Because of the processing backlog for unskilled workers, it is worth highlighting the difference between skilled and unskilled workers, again by way of an example from Allan Wernick.[27] Billy came to the United States from Trinidad as an F-1 student visa holder but soon tired of school and sought employment. He received a job as a chef's assistant in a 24-hour restaurant, working the 12:00 A.M. to 8:00 A.M. shift, which he held for two years. His employer then agreed to sponsor his immigrant petition, and Billy was granted labor certification because no U.S. worker was willing to take the graveyard shift. However, because the chef's assistant position fell under the unskilled worker category, the backlog for these visas was over fifteen years long.

Meanwhile, in the two years since his employer filed the first labor certification application, Billy was trained to bake the homemade pastries for which the restaurant was famous. A different restaurant then offered him a job as a pastry chef, based on his four years as chef's assistant and two years of training as a pastry chef. Billy was now qualified to do a job requiring at least two years of experience and hence could be considered a skilled worker. His new employer then filed a labor certification for him, which the U.S. Department of Labor approved; upon receipt, Billy was able to file for permanent residence, as there was no backlog for skilled workers from Trinidad at the time.

Fourth Preference. This category includes a diversity of "special immigrants"[28] that range from certain Panama Canal Zone employees, to juvenile dependents of a U.S. court who are eligible for foster care, to various religious workers.[29] Religious workers include ministers and other religious professionals, who may self-petition or be sponsored by the nonprofit organization that plans to employ them.[30]

Fifth Preference. This category is different from the other four in that those who qualify for these visas work as employer-investors, not as employees. Congress created this category to permit foreign nationals who create jobs in the United States to be able to immigrate. Current U.S. Citizenship and Immigration Services (USCIS) regulations require that qualifying individuals invest, or be in the process of investing, a minimum of $1 million; the minimum drops to $500,000 for those investing in a "targeted employment area"—one that has experienced high unemployment or is in a rural area.[31] Such investment must create jobs for at least ten "qualified employees," including U.S. citizens, LPRs, asylees, and refugees, but excluding the investor and his or her family.[32]

Just as in the family-sponsored preference categories, these employment-based immigrant visa groups have very specific requirements to which the prospective immigrant must adhere. Moreover, many of the categories require an additional step—labor certification—which is not a requirement of family-based immigration.

Refugees and Asylees

Aside from the family- and employment-based immigrant visa categories, the third major way noncitizens are able to immigrate is by qualifying for asylum. An individual who has received asylum or refugee status is eligible to apply for permanent residency after residing in the United States for one year.[33] Unlike voluntary family- and employment-based applicants, however, refugees and asylees are, by definition, involuntary migrants—they seek sanctuary in the United States for fear of persecution in their home country.

To qualify for asylum or refugee status, an individual must demonstrate a well-founded fear of persecution based on one of five specific grounds: race, religion, national origin, political opinion, or membership in a particular social group.[34] So, although you might hear this form of relief popularly referred to as "political asylum," one can receive asylum because of one's race or religion, for instance.[35] The main difference between an asylee and a refugee stems from where the petition originates: if the applicant is currently in another country (say, escapees from Darfur now living in Chad), then that person is applying for refugee status; if he or she is already within the United States, asylum is the proper remedy. Thus, refugees are processed for permanent resettlement in the United States by the Bureau of Population, Refugees, and Migration,[36] a division of the State Department; refugees receive legal status upon their arrival in the United States.

Many churches and other nonprofits work with the government to resettle refugees in their communities. In contrast, asylees do not obtain their status until they apply for it; the typical asylum applicant arrives at a U.S. airport or seaport on her own, often with few, fake, or no documents to identify her; an asylum officer or immigration judge receives her application for status.

To receive asylum or refugee status, one must prove a "well-founded fear of persecution." The applicant must show that he or she has suffered in the past, or will probably suffer in the future, persecution in the home country. This persecution must be on the basis of one of five grounds—race, religion, national origin, political opinion, or membership in a particular social group—and may not be based on purely economic hardship, acts of nature, or general civil strife. The applicant must demonstrate persecution at the hands of either the government or some nongovernmental actor that the local authorities were unable or unwilling to control, and demonstrate that he or she could not find some other town or city within the home country in which to safely resettle.[37]

Even if an asylum applicant is able to meet all these requirements, he or she is still subject to the discretion of the asylum officer or immigration judge reviewing the claim. This means that the officer or judge has the power to weigh the merits of the case against any negative factors—a minor criminal offense, say—and decide to deny the claim.

This brief discussion should alert you to the idea that obtaining an immigrant visa via the refugee or asylum route is no easy matter. As you might imagine, those involuntarily fleeing their homeland generally do not have time to collect the paperwork necessary to either enter the United States legally—a passport, for instance—or prove that they have a valid asylum claim once they arrive. This high bar to asylum is made more difficult by certain procedural rules passed by Congress in the mid-1990s, which you will learn about more in Chapter 3.

Diversity Visa Lottery Winners

An odd creature of U.S. immigration politics, the Diversity Visa lottery was intended to ensure that natives of low-admission nations were not overwhelmed by the large influx from Asia and Latin America following the abolition of the National Origins Quota system in 1965. Each year, the U.S. Department of State runs a lottery in which approximately 50,000 visas are issued to natives of low-admission states—countries from which fewer than 50,000 people have immigrated over the last five years. The State Department usually publishes a list of these low-admission states and the rules governing the admission process in August of each year at its website, http://travel.state.gov/visa/immigrants/types/types_1322.html.

Natives of these eligible nations need not be in the United States to apply, the entry form is rather short, and currently there is no fee for applying (although that may change in the future). While some noncitizens legally living in the United States fear that they may be deported if they apply and don't win, immigration specialist Allan Wernick notes that it is unlikely the immigration authorities will hunt them down; in any event, one has the option of using a mailing address other than one's home address on the entry form.[38] Undocumented persons, however, run the risk of exposing themselves to deportation because the lottery is not an amnesty, and therefore, those who have entered the United States without inspection and who win the lottery do not qualify for adjustment to LPR status.[39]

Nonimmigrants (Temporary Visitors)

Most noncitizens come to the United States not to immigrate, but to spend time here temporarily and for a specific purpose. Unlike immigrants, nonimmigrants do not intend to abandon their residences abroad or make the United States their home. Consequently, the visas that are granted to nonimmigrants limit what they may do while in the United States and how long they may stay.[40] These visas typically appear as a stamp on a passport, designating how long the nonimmigrant may stay in the United States, the visa's expiration date, and how many times the nonimmigrant may reenter the United States on the same visa.

The most common nonimmigrant visa categories are highlighted below.[41] In everyday parlance, you may often hear a nonimmigrant visa holder referred to by the statutory classification assigned to his or her status rather than to the kind of visa he or she holds. So, for instance, a student might be referred to as an "F-1 visa holder," which refers to the place in the immigration code that defines this classification: INA § 101(a)(15)(F)(1). You may find Figure 2.2 to be a helpful guide to the following discussion.

Figure 2.2   Nonimmigrants (Temporary Visitors)

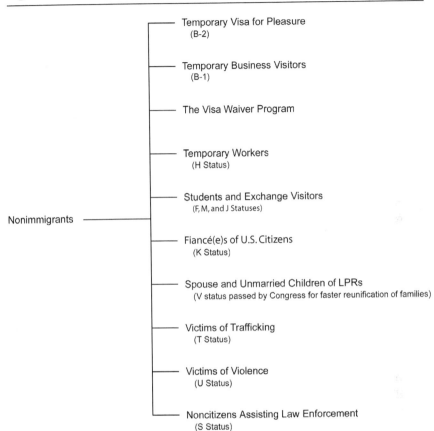

Nonimmigrants
- Temporary Visa for Pleasure (B-2)
- Temporary Business Visitors (B-1)
- The Visa Waiver Program
- Temporary Workers (H Status)
- Students and Exchange Visitors (F, M, and J Statuses)
- Fiancé(e)s of U.S. Citizens (K Status)
- Spouse and Unmarried Children of LPRs (V status passed by Congress for faster reunification of families)
- Victims of Trafficking (T Status)
- Victims of Violence (U Status)
- Noncitizens Assisting Law Enforcement (S Status)

Temporary Visitor for Pleasure (B-2)

The B-2 visa allows a foreign person to come to the United States temporarily for personal reasons other than to work or study.[42] Sometimes referred to as a "tourist visa," the B-2 also allows nonimmigrants to visit the United States for medical treatment; to attend a funeral, graduation, or some other important event; or simply to visit family and friends. Visas are typically valid for six months at a time but may be extended for up to a year upon application.

Temporary Business Visitors (B-1)

The B-1 visa specifically permits one to temporarily do business in the United States but not be employed by a U.S. company.[43] Examples of activities that qualify under this category include (1) organizing trade or negotiating a contract for a foreign company; (2) conducting independent research or engaging in other academic activity; (3) participating in an athletic event; and (4) investigating investment possibilities. B-1 visa holders are typically admitted for ninety days, although they may enjoy a longer visit if they demonstrate a need.

The Visa Waiver Program (VWP)

The Visa Waiver Program (VWP) allows citizens of some countries to enter the United States for ninety days for tourism or business without first obtaining the B-2 or B-1 visa. Run by the State Department, the VWP is open primarily to countries whose citizens have a solid track record for complying with nonimmigrant visa rules, countries that have sufficiently stringent security measures for the issuance of passports and travel documents, and countries that reciprocally offer visa-free travel to U.S. citizens. As of this writing, almost all of them are western European nations, plus Japan, Singapore, New Zealand, Brunei, and Australia. Updated information about the VWP may be found at http://www.travel.state.gov/visa/temp/without/without_1990.html#2.

Temporary Workers (H status)

Two categories of H visa[44] workers are worth highlighting: the H-1 status for professionals, and the H-2 status for unskilled laborers. The spouse and unmarried children under age twenty-one of an H visa holder may receive H-4 visas to accompany him or her.

The most common temporary work visa for professionals is the H-1B. Valid for an initial three-year period and renewable up to a maximum of six years, the H-1B is available to those who possess a four-year college degree or the equivalent in education and experience. One must have a job offer and a commitment from the employer to file an H-1B petition on the noncitizen's behalf. The job must be one for which a four-year degree is typically required; examples are schoolteacher, lawyer, architect, and engineer. The visa is not portable, however; should a new or second employer enter the picture, this employer must file a separate H-1B petition.

Aside from filing the H-1B petition, the employer must also get a Labor Condition Application (LCA) certified by the U.S. Department of Labor. The LCA parallels the labor certification process required to be filed with some employment-based immigrant petitions but is less burdensome. Instead of requiring the employer to demonstrate the lack of qualified U.S. workers to take the job, the LCA attests only that the employer has offered the job at a wage higher than the prevailing or actual wage, under the prevailing working conditions for current employees in the same job, and has conspicuously posted notice of filing the H-1B petition. The H-1B visa holder's spouse and unmarried children under age twenty-one are eligible to receive H-4 visas allowing them to travel to, but not work in, the United States.

One variant on the H-1B theme is based on specific free trade agreements the United States has entered into with other nations. Canadian and Mexican nationals may receive TN temporary work visas, while Singaporean and Chilean citizens may receive H-1B1 status. Most professionals from TN and H-1B1 countries have the option of choosing between these and the H-1B status. One key advantage of the TN and H-1B1 visas is that they are not subject to the six-year H-1B limit but may be renewed indefinitely. However, TN visa holders are not entitled to the prevailing wage, unlike H-1Bs and H-1B1s.

Paralleling the employment-based immigrant categories, the H nonimmigrant visa class likewise has a provision for temporary lesser skilled labor (H-2), apart from its benefits for professionals (H-1). H-2 visa holders are divided into two groups: H-2A visas are issued to agricultural workers; H-2B visas, to nonagricultural workers.

Because of the seasonal nature of agricultural work, many U.S. farmers and operators find it necessary to hire temporary migrant labor. In petitioning workers under the H-2A category, employers must demonstrate that they have attempted to recruit domestic labor[45] but are still in need of more help. H-2A visa holders may not remain in the United States longer than three years,[46] although they may seek approval to work in more than one temporary agricultural position.

H-2B visa holders may enter the United States to work only in temporary, not permanent, nonagricultural positions.[47] As such, a temporary staffing service that has a permanent need for persons with particular skills may not fill the job by hiring an H-2B visa holder.[48] Like H-2A visa holders, H-2B recipients may remain in the United States for the duration of the approved petition, up to a maximum of three years.[49]

Students and Exchange Visitors (F, M, and J)
International students and scholars may typically receive one of three
visa types: (1) the F-1 is the most common visa for those in college or
university programs (and, less commonly, it is available for those attending private elementary and secondary schools); (2) the M-1 is
specifically for those in community college and vocational schools;
and (3) J-1 visas are exchange visitor visas, and are also available to
foreign students. I will focus primarily on the pros and cons of the
F-1 and J-1 statuses, since these are the most common visas that international students acquire.

For either the F-1 or J-1 visa, the student must have been accepted
by a school, college, or university accredited by the U.S. Citizenship
and Immigration Services (USCIS) to accept noncitizens. Both visa
types permit the holder to complete his or her studies toward a degree; therefore, rather than specifying a length of stay, these visas are
typically valid for the "duration of status"—that is, until the holders
receive their degrees. Thus, it is no surprise to find international students at the same college enrolled in the same four-year degree program possessing one or the other of these visas; indeed, my college
roommate and I serve as a good example: I was from the Philippines
and had an F-1 visa; he was from Bolivia and had a J-1.

As to be expected from their different designations, there are three
essential differences between the F-1 and J-1 that relate to (1) the
funding required to support the student; (2) the possibility of employment while attending school; and (3) the opportunities for additional training in the United States. First, F-1 student visa holders
must demonstrate that they have sufficient private funds to support
their matriculation and living expenses for their first year of study in
the United States. These funds can include those from family and
friends, as well as any financial support that the college or university
can give in the form of grants or private loans. J-1 students, in contrast, come to the United States under the sponsorship of an exchange program approved by the State Department. As such, J-1 students typically receive substantial funding from public funds,
whether from the U.S. government or their home nation.

Second, F-1 student visa holders may typically work only on cam-
pus during their time at school and then only for a specific number of
hours a week; J-1 students may seek work off-campus for the program sponsor or another designated employer. Similarly, family
members with J-2 status accompanying the J-1 holder may also ob-

tain permission to work for their own support or to pay for recreational activities; they may not support the J-1 student.[50] F-2 family members, in contrast, may not work.

Third, F-1 student visa holders may engage in optional practical training (OPT) for up to twelve months in a field directly related to their area of study.[51] This OPT must be approved by the USCIS upon recommendation of the school and may be used while school is in session, during the summers, or upon completion of the degree. J-1 students, in contrast, are generally required to return to their home country for two years upon completing their degree.[52] The idea is that as an exchange student, the J-1 visitor will return to aid his or her home country through the benefits of his or her training and education.

Fiancé(e)s of U.S. Citizens (K)

The K visa may be used by a U.S. citizen to bring one's foreign fiancé/fiancée or spouse to the United States; K visas are not available to spouses of LPRs, nor are they available to persons currently in the United States. In a sense, the K visa is much closer to an immigrant visa than a nonimmigrant one because the foreign partner typically intends to join the citizen spouse permanently in the United States.

The K-1 fiancé(e) visa allows U.S. citizens to bring their fiancé(e)s to the United States for a period of ninety days, during which time the couple must legally marry. After marriage, the noncitizen spouse may adjust to permanent residence status. The K visa may only be issued abroad; should the marriage fall through, the noncitizen is required to return home before being eligible to apply for another nonimmigrant or immigrant visa. For example, a person who arrives on a fiancé(e) visa but then gets cold feet may not change status to an H-1B temporary worker even if there is a firm willing and able to petition her; she would have to return to her home country and have the firm file a new H-1B petition on her behalf. Minor unmarried children of K-1 visa holders may receive the K-2 visa to accompany their parents.

The K-3 spouse visa benefits foreign spouses who are waiting for their immediate relative petitions to be processed but are experiencing delays. The K-3 visa allows the spouse to be with his or her U.S. citizen counterpart in relatively short order. The main disadvantage, though, is that it may take longer for the noncitizen to achieve LPR status than if the U.S. citizen were to directly file an immediate relative petition. This is because once the K-3 spouse arrives in the

United States, he or she has to then apply for adjustment to LPR status, a process that would take longer than if he or she had stayed in the home country and his/her U.S. citizen spouse had filed an immediate relative petition directly on his/her behalf.[53]

Spouse and Unmarried Children of LPRs (V)

As was discussed earlier in this chapter, the immigration code devotes only the single, second-preference family-sponsored visa category to LPRs who want to bring their families to the United States. Consequently, the waiting period for these spouses and minor children is usually very long, resulting in the separation of families for many years. In an attempt to reunify families, Congress in 2000 passed legislation creating the V-1 (spouse) and V-2 (child) visa for relatives of LPRs who filed second-preference family-sponsored petitions on their behalf on or before December 21, 2000.[54]

Victims of Trafficking (T) and Violence (U) and Noncitizens Assisting Law Enforcement (S)

Congress has seen fit to create three visa classifications for noncitizens who assist law enforcement agents. The T visa is awarded to victims of severe trafficking who are willing to assist law enforcement agents in apprehending the perpetrators; similarly, the U visa is available to victims of domestic violence who agree to provide assistance to the government. Both T and U visa holders are allowed to adjust their status to that of LPR after three years. The S—"snitch"—visa is available to those who supply critical information to law enforcement agencies and whose presence in the United States is deemed essential to the prosecution of the crime. S visa holders may also apply for adjustment, but under more limited circumstances.[55]

As suggested in the preceding discussion, it is possible for nonimmigrants to change their visa status. Briefly, a nonimmigrant is allowed to do one of three things: (1) *extend* his or her visa status, which would apply when a student fails to complete her degree in typical fashion and requires an extension to complete a thesis, for example; (2) *change* his or her status from one nonimmigrant classification to another—upon graduation, a college student receiving sponsorship from an employer may receive a temporary work permit (usually the H-1B); or (3) *adjust* his or her status from nonimmigrant to immigrant—a student who marries a U.S. citizen may adjust his or her status from F-1 to LPR.

Removal from the United States (Inadmissibility and Deportability)

I have now explored the ways by which noncitizens may come to the United States permanently as immigrants or temporarily as nonimmigrants, and the different categories Congress has created for each group. Fitting the appropriate visa category is only the first step, however. Congress has also created elaborate rules to ensure, in theory, that admitting these individuals into the United States will not detrimentally affect those already residing here. Analogously, there are also rules that are designed to remove noncitizens who are already here if they engage in activity that runs contrary to national interests. A quick example of such an undesirable person would be the terrorist or criminal; even if my brother qualifies for admission under the fourth-preference family-sponsored category, he should not be allowed entry if he's a terrorist.

The rules regarding when a person may be barred from entering the United States are called "inadmissibility" rules;[56] those that govern when one must leave are "deportability"[57] provisions. Just as was done with the visa categories above, the substantive law that governs these rules will be highlighted, leaving any procedural questions to Chapter 3. The goal here is to understand what reasons the United States might have for denying an otherwise qualified person entry or requiring him or her to leave.

Inadmissibility and Deportability

Before I begin, here's an important note: a noncitizen facing a deportation[58] charge should seriously consider consulting a lawyer because the consequences of being forced to leave the United States are often quite severe. Even though a removal hearing is a civil administrative proceeding for which representation by counsel is not required, noncitizens for whom it is important to remain in the United States— because of family or business ties to U.S. citizens, for instance— should hire an experienced immigration attorney to represent them before the immigration judge. Although no right to a free attorney at immigration proceedings exists, several nonprofit organizations and law school legal clinics provide such assistance to those who qualify. I have listed some of these organizations in Chapter 5.

Crimes

If there is one thing most Americans agree about, it is that noncitizens who commit crimes either should not be allowed into the country or should be deported. Where the disagreement lies, however, is in what *kinds* of crimes should render someone removable. Because federal immigration law sets forth rules regarding deportability that are different from regular federal and state criminal law, many noncitizens who face relatively minor criminal charges end up being deported. It is paramount that if you ever are faced with a criminal charge, the defense lawyer that you employ is fully aware of the immigration consequences of that charge and advises you accordingly. Many a criminal defense attorney has advised a noncitizen client to plead to some lesser-included offense to avoid jail time and expense, not realizing that this plea simultaneously consigns the client to deportation. Finding a criminal defense lawyer who has represented noncitizens on a regular basis is crucial.

Moral Turpitude Crimes

Noncitizens who commit "crimes involving moral turpitude" are both generally inadmissible and deportable—that is, they can be barred from entering the United States, and they may be removed from the United States if already here. Although difficult to define with precision, moral turpitude crimes are those that society typically finds have a certain depravity or repugnance to them. Theft and violent crimes usually qualify as crimes involving moral turpitude.[59]

As you might imagine, the rules regarding when a moral turpitude crime constitutes a reason to deport are generally considered more favorable to the noncitizen than those that bar him or her from entry. For instance, a person may be inadmissible simply for having *admitted* to committing a moral turpitude crime,[60] but to be deportable, (1) that same person must have been *convicted* of the crime, (2) the crime must have been committed *within five years of admission*, and (3) the crime must have been *punishable by at least a yearlong sentence*.[61] The reason for this difference reflects Congress's realization that a longtime resident who faces deportation likely has developed more important ties to the United States than the first-time entrant; therefore, Congress requires the immigration authorities to comply with a more stringent set of rules before it allows them to remove an individual already in the United States.

Drug Crimes

The United States has been waging the so-called war on drugs for decades, and part of this battle acknowledges the role that noncitizens play in the transport and distribution of drugs across borders and within the United States itself. The inadmissibility bar based on drug crimes is a particularly high hurdle: any noncitizen who has been convicted of, admits to having committed, or admits to committing acts that constitute the essential elements of[62] a drug crime (including conspiracy or attempt) under U.S., state, or foreign law is inadmissible.[63] The analogous deportability ground is limited to actual drug crime *convictions* and specifically excludes individuals who have been convicted of one count of possession of 30 grams or less of marijuana for personal use; drug abusers or addicts remain deportable.[64]

Aggravated Felonies

Perhaps no other criminal removal ground has gained more academic and popular attention than the immigration code's definition of an "aggravated felony." Having an "aggravated felony" conviction is a deportability ground[65] as well as a likely bar to citizenship.[66] While Congress's decision not to include "aggravated felonies" as bars to admission may appear anomalous, this omission may well be because the current crime-based inadmissibility grounds are sufficiently strict that "aggravated felons" would not be able to enter anyway.

Although broader in scope than both moral turpitude and drug crimes, "aggravated felonies" are particularly serious ones that typically include drug or violent offenses.[67] Since the term was introduced in 1988, the definition of *aggravated felony* has grown tremendously to now include such crimes as the sexual abuse of a minor, child pornography, forgery, obstruction of justice, racketeering offenses, and crimes of violence.[68]

Because state crimes can trigger federal deportation, a constant source of litigation of late has been over what state misdemeanors qualify as "aggravated felonies" under the immigration code to render a person deportable. For instance, courts across the country are currently divided over whether vehicle burglaries are crimes of violence under the "aggravated felony" statute; until the Supreme Court resolves this issue, the same conduct arising out of different states will lead to different outcomes; some of those convicted will be deported, and some will not.[69]

Terrorism

Since September 11, 2001, the United States has been particularly sensitive about the relationship between terrorism and immigration. Although the overwhelming majority of noncitizens in this country are neither criminals nor terrorists, because all of the 9/11 hijackers were noncitizens, Congress and the Bush administration have expanded the definition of *terrorist activity*[70] to encompass actions one would not usually associate with terrorism. Immigration scholar Legomsky, for instance, wonders whether some acts of "youthful vandalism" may fall under these prohibitions if the damage is deemed "substantial."[71] As with criminal charges, terrorism allegations also warrant consultation with an experienced attorney.

Aside from the inclusion of terrorism as a basis for both exclusion and deportation,[72] perhaps more notable has been the use of other immigration requirements to track terrorist suspects. For instance, the government has made full use of its powers to require the registration of noncitizens to conduct interviews and detentions of thousands of Arabs and Muslims after 9/11.[73] Immigrant communities, who have no desire to house terrorists themselves, have urged federal officials to work cooperatively with them instead of vilifying their members, a strategy that has seemed more satisfactory to both the government and the noncitizen groups.

Political Activity

Those who have been members of a totalitarian or communist party, based in either the United States or abroad, are inadmissible, although not deportable.[74] While this may seem a relic of the Cold War era, these provisions are still on the books, although exclusions based on these grounds are far less common today.[75]

Other Immigration Violations
Document Fraud and Failure to Register

Noncitizens who commit fraud, from submitting false immigration documents to making material misrepresentations to obtain true ones, are inadmissible.[76] Similarly, those who fail to register changes of address with the immigration authorities, who engage in document fraud, or who falsely claim citizenship are deportable.[77] *Document fraud* is therefore a broad term, and it encompasses activities as diverse as procuring a false passport or visa, engaging in marriage fraud[78] to obtain immediate relative status, or falsifying a U.S. birth certificate. As hinted at earlier, this question of document fraud becomes a particular challenge in asylum cases, where a person may have a valid claim but may also have left his or her country and attempted to enter this one using false travel documents.

Unlawful Presence

The term *unlawful presence* applies to noncitizens (1) who have been admitted and then stay beyond the time they are allowed, thereby making their presence unlawful; or (2) who have entered without having been admitted or paroled into the United States.[79] Those who have stayed longer than permitted are sometimes referred to as "overstays." Persons who have come here without the proper documents—so-called undocumented migrants, sometimes pejoratively called "illegal aliens"—will be discussed separately, although they are technically a subset of those persons who are here unlawfully.[80]

After one's visa expires, he or she generally enjoys a six-month grace period before the "unlawful presence" provisions kick in. In other words, a nonimmigrant who leaves the United States within six months of when her visa expires will likely not be barred from reentering despite the fact that she was in the United States without a valid visa for several months. Austin Fragomen and Steven Bell warn, however, that immigration authorities are currently of the view that H-1B (temporary professional workers) who are terminated from work enjoy no grace period,[81] and so it likely behooves all nonimmigrants to try to secure their departure from the United States as close to their visa end date as possible. In any event, those who stay longer than six months and then leave *are* barred from reentering for three years; if one overstays beyond one year, one is barred for ten years from reentry.[82]

Health Concerns and the Special Case of HIV/AIDS
Noncitizens with serious communicable diseases are barred from entering the United States. Although HIV/AIDS is not communicable via casual contact, Congress has decided it poses enough of a national health risk to specifically list it as a disease of concern, barring those with HIV/AIDS from entering the country.[83] Other grounds for inadmissibility for health-related reasons include physical and mental disorders that render one a danger to others, as well as drug abuse and addiction. In addition, an admitted noncitizen may be deportable if he or she fails to abide by any medical conditions imposed by the U.S. Department of Health and Human Services.[84]

Public Charge
Pending immigrants who are likely to go on public welfare are inadmissible;[85] those who go on welfare within five years of entry are deportable.[86] Examples of "means-tested" benefits that render one a public charge are food stamps and Medicaid.[87] While those applying for asylee or refugee status are exempted, this inadmissibility ground makes it very difficult for poorer immigrants, especially since the Personal Responsibility and Work Opportunity Reconciliation Act of 1996[88] made the affidavits of support signed by sponsors in the United States binding, enforceable contracts, should the beneficiary-immigrants become public charges. Back to an earlier example: if I filed an affidavit of support on my Filipino brother's behalf in conjunction with his immigrant petition, and he later becomes a public charge, the U.S. government has a right to seek reimbursement of these public welfare benefits directly from me.

Undocumented Migrants
Because they have been the focus of so much recent anti-immigrant legislation, it is useful to discuss undocumented migrants separately from overstays and others who have been unlawfully present in the United States. Noncitizens who arrive without being duly inspected by immigration authorities—for example, those who cross the U.S.-Canada border illegally, or who stow away on a U.S.-bound vessel—are inadmissible.[89] Analogously, those who successfully evade inspection but then are apprehended are deportable for being inadmissible when they entered and may be criminally liable as well.[90]

Because Congress considers undocumented migrants to be inadmissible rather than deportable, it effectively treats them as an exception to the rule that noncitizens in the United States receive more protections from deportation than do new entrants. Whereas Congress generally assumes that those already living in the United States have ties to the country that require that the government deport them only with good reason, Congress does not make the same assumption with respect to undocumented migrants. Thus, undocumented migrants who are caught at a border are summarily removed under an expedited procedure, while those who are found within the United States are charged under more stringent inadmissibility, rather than deportability, grounds at their removal hearing before the immigration judge.[91]

Relief from Removal

Notwithstanding the various inadmissibility and deportability grounds described earlier, Congress recognizes that there are some instances in which noncitizens should be allowed to enter and remain in the United States. Steve Legomsky describes two forms of relief available—"lasting" and "limited."[92] I will now describe each in more detail.

Lasting Relief

Citizenship as a Defense to Removal. U.S. citizens are not subject to immigration law, and as such, cannot be deported. Therefore, the government must have to prove that one is a noncitizen before being able to remove that individual from the United States. Citizenship becomes, then, the ultimate defense against removal. Sometimes a person may have been a U.S. citizen at birth without having known it. If that person had been in deportation proceedings and proof of his or her U.S. citizenship came to light, the immigration judge would be required to halt the proceedings, regardless of whether the person had always thought of him- or herself as a noncitizen. Aside from not being deportable, U.S. citizens enjoy a whole host of other rights, including the right to vote, hold government jobs that LPRs cannot, and live outside the United States without losing permanent residence status.[93]

U.S. citizenship may be acquired in two ways: at birth and after birth. Citizenship at birth is obtained either by being born on U.S.

soil or by having parents who are U.S. citizens. Even if a person carries a foreign passport and has lived most of her life outside the United States but has at least one U.S. parent and certain other conditions exist, she may already be a U.S. citizen. Citizenship after birth occurs through naturalization—the typical case is when a foreign national arrives in the United States as an LPR, and then five years later applies to become a U.S. citizen.[94] Aside from the five-year residence requirement (three years for spouses of U.S. citizens), most citizenship applicants must (1) demonstrate physical presence in the United States for half of the five (or three) years here; (2) be of good moral character; (3) have a basic knowledge of U.S. government and history; (4) be able to read, write, and speak simple English (not a requirement for some older immigrants); (5) be eighteen years of age or older; and (6) express allegiance to the U.S. government.[95] Recently, the U.S. government decided to raise the application fee for citizenship while also restructuring the civics test, prompting some civil rights groups to protest that these changes would deter many otherwise eligible, poorer immigrants from naturalizing. Apparently, the United States is not alone: in 2007, Australia, France, and England modified their entry requirements for would-be immigrants to reflect cultural or language skills each country values.[96]

Registry. To eliminate the harsh effects of deportation on long-time resident noncitizens, including those undocumented migrants who entered the United States without inspection, Congress will grant LPR status to those who entered here before the registry date, which is currently January 1, 1972. Registry creates a record of lawful admission where there was none; eligible noncitizens must also demonstrate continuous residence since their arrival and good moral character.[97] As you can imagine, not many undocumented persons currently in the United States have lived here long enough to qualify for the registry; even if they have, they may find it difficult to prove their presence here since 1972.

Cancellation of Removal. A person facing deportation or removal may ask the immigration judge to grant him a form of relief called "cancellation of removal."[98] This remedy allows the noncitizen either to keep his LPR status or, if he is a nonimmigrant, to adjust to LPR status. The result is that the noncitizen who receives cancellation of removal is placed in the same stead as a regular LPR. It should be no surprise, then, that an immigration judge has complete discretion whether to grant or deny a request for cancellation of removal. The judge weighs the positives and negatives of the noncitizen's case to decide whether relief would be appropriate.

Noncitizen LPRs qualify for cancellation of removal if they (1) have been an LPR for not less than five years; (2) have resided in the United States continuously for seven years after having been admitted in any status, including a nonimmigrant status; and (3) have not been convicted of an aggravated felony.[99] Only if all three conditions are met will the noncitizen be able to have the judge exercise his or her discretionary power to grant or deny relief. If it is granted, the noncitizen's LPR status is fully restored.

Nonimmigrants qualify for cancellation of removal—and adjustment to LPR status—if they (1) have been continuously physically present in the United States for at least ten years; (2) have been persons of good moral character; (3) have not been convicted of any moral turpitude, drug, or fraud crimes; and (4) have established that their removal would cause an exceptional and extreme unusual hardship to the noncitizen's spouse, parent, or child who is a U.S. citizen or LPR.[100] As with the first, this second form of relief requires a favorable exercise of the immigration judge's discretion.

Amnesty. From time to time, Congress has enacted laws that have allowed longtime undocumented migrants to adjust to LPR status upon the fulfillment of certain conditions, such as proving that they have lived continuously in the United States for a certain number of years and are willing to pay a fine. The most recent large-scale amnesty program was signed into law by President Ronald Reagan in 1986 as part of the Immigration Reform and Control Act (IRCA).[101] In the spring terms of 2006 and 2007, Congress debated—and President George W. Bush supported—possibly enacting a work program that would allow some undocumented workers to eventually apply for LPR status. That proposal was not passed into law.

Statutory Exceptions. For each of the different grounds of inadmissibility and deportability, Congress has also created exceptions. For example, a single crime of moral turpitude committed by a noncitizen while still a minor will not bar that individual from entry if this crime was committed more than five years from the date of application for a visa.[102] Unfortunately, there are no clear patterns as to when an exception will apply. For instance, the exception for minors that was noted earlier applies only to moral turpitude crimes, but not to drug offenses.[103] Instead of trying to catalog the myriad exceptions for the various removal grounds here, should a particular ground appear to apply to your situation, make sure to consult an experienced immigration attorney about the possible exceptions that may apply.

Discretionary Waivers. Like exceptions, discretionary waivers are also available for violations of the inadmissibility and deportability grounds. Unlike exceptions, however, Congress has delegated the decision as to whether to excuse a noncitizen's violation to the discretion of the federal government, usually through a cabinet official, such as the Secretary of Homeland Security. Through promulgated regulations, the official then delegates the task of deciding individual cases to immigration officers or judges. As such, even though a noncitizen may qualify for certain relief, she may not receive it if the official reviewing her case decides not to grant it. For example, immigration officers at the border have the discretion to waive many of the inadmissibility grounds for nonimmigrants,[104] presumably because unlike LPRs, nonimmigrants are only in the United States for a brief period. As with the exceptions, there are no clear patterns as to when discretionary waivers are available, so please consult an immigration attorney about these as well.

Given the current climate against undocumented migration and overstay, one particular waiver worth noting is the "extreme hardship waiver," used to overcome the three- and ten-year bars to admission against those whose unlawful presence in the United States has been significant. In such cases, the noncitizen facing removal must prove that a U.S. citizen or LPR spouse or parent will suffer "extreme hardship" should the deportation ensue; hardship to children does not qualify.[105] Sadness attendant on separation does not count, although severe medical, financial, or personal circumstances might.[106]

Limited Relief

Parolees. Parolees are those persons the immigration service allows, for humanitarian reasons, to be under temporary, supervised release into the United States.[107] These are individuals whom the government has not allowed to enter but does not want to detain pending their removal, or those who have yet to receive a decision on their admission. Aside from the Cuban Marielitos we met in Chapter 1, the most infamous recent parolee was then-six-year-old Elián González, over whom there was much debate about whether he should receive political asylum in the United States or be returned to Cuba. The government eventually returned Elián to Cuba to rejoin his father there.

An important variation on this theme is "advanced parole." Noncitizens legally in the United States who want to leave for a brief time but also want to ensure their return should seek advanced parole, essentially permission to return to the United States and be paroled in, pending consideration of their admissibility. While it would be more desirable for the noncitizen to actually be admitted upon return, advanced parole guarantees that the noncitizen will not have wasted his or her resources attempting a reentry into the United States, only to be denied admission. Of course, advanced parole may be revoked if the noncitizen violates an admissibility rule other than not having the requisite immigration documents—the commission of a crime of moral turpitude, for instance, would void the advanced parole grant.[108]

Temporary Protected Status (TPS). Temporary Protected Status (TPS) is the nonimmigrant analog to a grant of asylum or refugee status. In order to provide temporary protection to citizens of countries torn by civil strife or natural disaster, the Secretary of Homeland Security may designate a country for TPS, permitting its nationals to apply for protection and nonimmigrant status. Although it does not convey LPR status upon grantees, TPS protection allows one to change to another nonimmigrant status or to LPR status if one qualifies on some other ground, like marriage to a U.S. citizen.[109]

Now that we know the basic substance of immigration law—those reasons why noncitizens are permitted to enter and why they may be required to leave—I shift focus in Chapter 3 to the procedures that govern its creation and implementation.

Notes

1. See INA §§ 101 et seq., which can be found at 8 U.S. Code §§ 1101 et seq.

2. Austin T. Fragomen Jr. and Steven C. Bell, *Immigration Fundamentals: A Guide to Law and Practice,* 4th ed. (New York: Practicing Law Institute, 2004), 5-67.

3. The one quirky exception to this rule is that immediate relatives cannot bring their family members with them as derivative beneficiaries; they must file separate petitions for these family members after they have arrived in the United States. Immediate relatives are described more fully in the section on family-sponsored immigration.

4. INA § 201(b).

5. Same-gender partners are not "spouses" under the INA. *Adams v. Howerton,* 673 F.2d 1036 (9th Cir. 1982). Congress's Defense of Marriage Act also forbids same-gender couples from receiving any federal benefits, which would include immigration benefits, by limiting the definition of *marriage* to unions between a man and a woman. See Pub. L. 104-199, codified at 1 U.S.C. § 7 (1996)

6. *Child* is a term of art in immigration law and is defined by INA § 101(b)(1) to include stepchildren and adopted children as well as biological children.

7. A U.S. citizen wanting to petition his or her parent to immigrate must be at least twenty-one years old. INA § 201(b).

8. For more detail on employment-based visas, see Daniel Weissbrodt and Laura Danielson, *Immigration Law and Procedure,* 5th ed. (St. Paul, MN: Thomson West, 2005), ch. 5, § 5-3.1(b), which contains a concise, readable description of each preference category. Allan Wernick, *U.S. Immigration and Citizenship: Your Complete Guide,* 4th ed. (Cincinnati: Emmis, 2004), ch. 3, provides many specific hypothetical examples of immigrants who would or would not qualify for certain visas. My discussion here borrows heavily, and sometimes directly, from theirs.

9. INA § 101(a)(44).

10. Stephen H. Legomsky, *Immigration and Refugee Law and Policy*, 4th ed. (New York: Foundation Press, 2005), 293.

11. 56 Fed. Reg. 60897-01.

12. Wernick, *U.S. Immigration and Citizenship,* 34.

13. 8 CFR § 204.5.

14. Wernick, *U.S. Immigration and Citizenship,* 36.

15. Ira J. Kurzban, *Immigration Law Sourcebook,* 9th ed. (Washington, DC: American Immigration Law Foundation, 2004), 686.

16. 8 CFR § 204.5(k)(2).

17. INA § 203(b)(2).

18. See, e.g., *Lee v. INS,* 407 F.2d 1110 (9th Cir. 1969) (upholding finding that Lee did not possess exceptional ability as musician).

19. Wernick, *U.S. Immigration and Citizenship,* 40.

20. INA § 203(b)(2)(B)(ii).

21. INA § 101(a)(31).

22. 8 CFR § 204.5(k)(2).

23. 8 CFR § 204.5(l)(2).

24. I do not mean to use the term *unskilled* as pejorative; obviously, anyone who works brings skills to the job. Rather, it is a term of art to distinguish the differences in education or experience required between job holders.

25. INA § 203(b)(3)(A)(iii). Thus, even if an immigrant has more than two years of experience, if the job requires less than two years he or she will be considered an unskilled worker. Fragomen and Bell, *Immigration Fundamentals*, 2-75.

26. Ibid., 2-76.

27. Wernick, *U.S. Immigration and Citizenship*, 39.

28. INA § 203(b)(4).

29. Notably, some of these subgroups—the juvenile dependents, for instance—are clearly neither employees nor employers, although they have been included in this category. This is yet another example of the confusing nature of immigration policy.

30. For more on the fourth preference category and on religious workers in particular, see Fragomen and Bell, *Immigration Fundamentals*, 2-87 to 2-90. Note that while *ministers* may apply at any time, other religious workers were required to apply by September 30, 2008. Ibid., 2-89.

31. 8 CFR § 204.6(f).

32. Ibid.

33. INA § 209(a)(1)(B).

34. INA § 101(a)(42).

35. Wernick, *U.S. Immigration and Citizenship*, 201.

36. For basic information on this bureau, see http://www.state.gov/g/prm/ (last visited on Mar. 13, 2008).

37. For more on the basic requirements of proving an asylum claim, see the Board of Immigration Appeals' 1985 decision in *In re Acosta*, 19 I. & N. 211.

38. Wernick, *U.S. Immigration and Citizenship*, 45.

39. See the advocacy group Immigration Equality's website, "Most Common Questions Asked of Immigration Equality," http://www.immigrationequality.org/template.php?pageid=27.

40. Wernick, *U.S. Immigration and Citizenship*, 138.

41. INA § 101(a)(15) contains the complete list of all the nonimmigrant visa categories.

42. INA § 101(a)(15)(B)(2).

43. INA § 101(a)(15)(B)(1). A related business visa is the L-1 intracompany transferee, referred to in one of the earlier examples in the text. This visa is useful for those managerial employees of a foreign company assigned to do work for a subsidiary based in the United States. INA § 101(a)(15)(L)(1).

44. INA § 101(a)(15)(H).

45. INA § 216.

46. 8 CFR § 214.2(h)(5).

47. *Matter of Artee Corp.*, 18 I. & N. Dec. 366 (Comm'r 1982).

48. Weissbrodt and Danielson, *Immigration Law and Procedure*, 164.

49. 8 CFR § 214.2(h)(13).

50. 8 CFR § 214.2(j)(1).

51. 8 CFR § 214.2(f)(10).

52. INA § 212(e).

53. Wernick, *U.S. Immigration and Citizenship*, 185.

54. Fragomen and Bell, *Immigration Fundamentals*, 5-252 to 5-253.

55. Ibid., 5-243 to 5-246 (S visa); 5-251 to 5-252 (T and U visas).

56. INA § 212.

57. INA § 237.

58. While being denied a visa or entry into the United States is certainly a disability, the consequences of that denial are usually less severe, especially if one is not facing persecution or extreme hardship in one's home country.

59. Wernick, *U.S. Immigration and Citizenship*, 63.

60. Even more stringently, a person who has admitted committing the acts constituting the essential elements of the crime is likewise inadmissible. INA § 212(a)(2)(A)(i).

61. Compare INA § 212(a)(2)(A)(i)(I) (inadmissibility) with INA § 237(a)(2)(A)(i) (deportability).

62. This three-part "admission/commission of the act" language also applies to the moral turpitude crime bar. INA § 212(a)(2)(A)(i).

63. INA § 212(a)(2)(A)(i)(II). The term of art used is *controlled substance crime*.

64. INA § 237(a)(2)(B)(i) and (ii).

65. INA § 237(a)(2)(A)(iii).

66. One necessary requirement for citizenship is that one has displayed "good moral character" for the required statutory period (three or five years). Having an "aggravated felony" on one's record will almost certainly disqualify a person if it is within the statutory period. And even if it occurred many years ago, the noncitizen still is unlikely to become a citizen because he or she will be subject to deportation for having committed an aggravated felony. See Wernick, *U.S. Immigration and Citizenship*, 98.

67. Ibid.

68. INA § 101(a)(43).

69. Legomsky, *Immigration and Refugee Law and Policy*, 561.

70. See INA § 212(a)(3)(B) for the full, lengthy description of terrorist activities and organizations.

71. Legomsky, *Immigration and Refugee Law and Policy*, 431.

72. INA § 212(a)(3)(B) (inadmissibility); § 237(a)(4)(B) (deportability). You'll note that the deportability ground simply references the inadmissibility provisions in full.

73. See, e.g., David Cole, *Enemy Aliens: Double Standards and Constitutional Freedoms in the War on Terrorism* (New York: New Press, 2003).

74. Compare INA § 212(a)(3)(d)(i) (inadmissibility based on membership in totalitarian or communist party) with INA § 237(a)(4) (deportability is based on subversive activities).

75. Wernick, *U.S. Immigration and Citizenship*, 65.

76. INA § 212(a)(6)(c)(i) (misrepresentation); INA § 212(a)(7) (documentation requirements).

77. INA § 237(a)(3).

78. See also specifically INA § 237(a)(1)(G) (marriage fraud as deportability ground).

79. INA § 212(a)(9) (inadmissibility); § 237(a)(1)(A)–(C) (deportability).

80. INA § 212(a)(9)(B)(ii).

81. Fragomen and Bell, *Immigration Fundamentals*, 5-124 to 5-125.

82. INA § 212(a)(9)(B)(i)(I) and (II).

83. INA § 212(a)(1)(A). On July 16, 2008, the U.S. Senate voted to repeal the HIV/AIDS ban on entry; however, as of this writing, this version of the bill has not been formally approved by Congress or signed by the president, nor have enacting regulations been promulgated.

84. INA § 237(a)(1)(C)(ii).

85. INA § 212(a)(4).

86. INA § 237(a)(5).

87. Wernick, *U.S. Immigration and Citizenship*, 56.

88. Public Law 104-193, 110 Stat. 2105 (Aug. 22, 1996).

89. INA § 212(a)(6)(A)(i).

90. INA § 237(a)(1)(a). INA § 275(a)(1) makes entry without inspection a misdemeanor, while INA § 276(a) makes the reentry of a deported migrant a felony.

91. Kurzban, *Immigration Law Sourcebook*, 102.

92. Legomsky, *Immigration and Refugee Law and Policy*, 572–632 (ch. 8, "Relief from Deportability").

93. Wernick, *U.S. Immigration and Citizenship*, 89–90.

94. See generally Legomsky, *Immigration and Refugee Law and Policy*, 1265–1373 (ch. 13, "Citizenship"); and Wernick, *U.S. Immigration and Citizenship*, 87 et seq. (sec. II, "Naturalization and Citizenship").

95. Wernick, *U.S. Immigration and Citizenship*, 93.

96. Migration Information Source, "Top 10 Migration Issues of 2007," http://www.migrationinformation.org/pdf/MIS-Top-10-Migration-Issues-2007.pdf.

97. INA § 249; Weissbrodt and Danielson, *Immigration Law and Procedure*, 302.

98. INA § 240A.

99. INA § 240A(a).

100. INA § 240A(b)(1). There is also a parallel provision for battered spouses and children. INA § 240A(b)(2).

101. Pub. L. 99-603, 100 Stat. 3359 (Nov. 6, 1986).

102. INA § 212(a)(2)(A)(ii).

103. Ibid.

104. INA § 212(d)(3).

105. INA § 212(a)(9)(B)(5).

106. See Igbanugo Partners International Law Firm, "The Hardship Waiver: A Must-Have for Those with Time-Related Bars of Admissibility," October 2, 2007, available at http://www.mshale.com/article.cfm?articleID =1596 (last visited on Mar. 13, 2008).

107. INA § 212(d)(5) and IIRAIRA § 602.

108. Weissbrodt and Danielson, *Immigration Law and Procedure*, 301–302.

109. Ibid., 304–305.

3

Immigration
Procedure Basics

In Chapter 1 we learned that immigration law is like contract law: Congress determines the terms under which noncitizens are allowed to enter, and when they must exit, the United States. The central product of Congress's labors is the labyrinthine Immigration and Nationality Act (INA), the substance of which we explored in Chapter 2. Here in Chapter 3, I examine how immigration law is enforced.

You may recall that in Chapter 1, I noted that the federal executive branch, headed by the president, is in charge of implementing the INA. Because the president couldn't possibly attend to all the details of immigration enforcement, Congress has delegated enforcement authority to various administrative agencies. As its name suggests, an *administrative agency* develops the specific rules required to effectuate the broader policies Congress sets forth in the immigration code. For example, after Congress created the H-1B temporary worker visa for business professionals, the U.S. Citizenship and Immigration Services (USCIS) had to determine the steps an applicant and his or her employer must take in order to qualify for that visa, including the forms they must fill out, the supporting documents they must provide, and how many years the employee may hold that visa. Agency rules are typically found in the Code of Federal Regulations (CFR).

This chapter unfolds in five parts: the first section introduces you to the basic structure of the federal immigration system—what agency is responsible for enforcing what part of the immigration code. Whereas the Departments of Labor and Health and Human

Services deal specifically with noncitizens' employment and health issues, the Departments of State, Homeland Security, and Justice supervise a migrant's travel to and removal from the United States.

The second section describes the basic procedural rules that govern the admission and expulsion of noncitizens, including the many steps one must take to enter the United States, and then to remain, should the government seek to deport.

The third section examines the judiciary's role in overseeing Congress and the agencies. As was shown in Chapter 1, much of U.S. law leaves virtually absolute or "plenary" immigration power in the hands of Congress and the agencies, but federal courts still have a role to play in making sure that noncitizens are treated fairly, especially when federal agencies attempt to deport them.

The fourth section explores the growing role that state and local governments have sought to play in enforcing immigration policy. As the most recent census has revealed, immigrants are settling in larger numbers in states not historically known as immigrant receivers, such as South Carolina and Delaware.[1]

The final section of this chapter attempts to answer the million-dollar question, Do I need to get an attorney to help me with my immigration problem? As a general rule, many initial issues having to do with immigrant or nonimmigrant visas can be resolved without a lawyer's help, while problems involving the possible deportation of an individual should be addressed in consultation with counsel, assuming the noncitizen would like to find ways of remaining legally in the United States. In between seeking entry and avoiding deportation lie a host of other issues spanning the spectrum of legal complexity. Though undoubtedly an oversimplification, like most legal problems, the cost effectiveness of hiring a skilled immigration attorney will depend on weighing the benefits of acquiring or maintaining an immigration status against the cost of having to return to one's home country, factoring in the added value a skilled professional could bring to bear on the issue balanced against the cost of hiring an attorney. Typically, the stronger the ties a noncitizen develops with the United States—whether economic, cultural, or familial—the greater the desire to remain and the greater the willingness to pay for immigration advice. But, as with many things in life, one must carefully assess the experience of the so-called expert before paying his or her fee.

Introduction to the Federal Immigration Bureaucracy: The Administrative Apparatus

As Figure 3.1 shows, five federal departments help enforce Congress's immigration policy: the Department of State, the Department of Health and Human Services, the Department of Homeland Security, the Department of Labor, and the Department of Justice.[2]

Of these, the Department of Health and Human Services and the Department of Labor are perhaps the easiest to explain, as these offices are in charge of immigration issues related to each agency's primary mission. For instance, Health and Human Services administers health policies regarding tuberculosis as well as other diseases that may travel via immigration; similarly, the Labor Department oversees the immigration of employees to ensure that they are not taking jobs away from qualified U.S. workers.

The remaining three agencies, State, Homeland Security, and Justice, track the process through which noncitizens apply for admission, enter, and leave the United States. In brief, the State Department handles visa processing at consulates and embassies abroad, Homeland Security patrols the borders and keeps tabs on noncitizens while they are in the United States, and the Justice Department administers hearings for those accused of violating the terms of their stay.

For many noncitizens abroad, the first government officials they meet en route to America are at U.S. embassies or consulates, which are overseen by the State Department. Consular officers process and approve both nonimmigrant and immigrant visas, often after a personal interview. One must be careful to put one's best foot forward during the personal interview because there is virtually no review of a consular officer's denial of a visa application.

Visa in hand, the noncitizen seeking to enter the United States must undergo an inspection at the airport, seaport, or land border by an immigration officer of the U.S. Customs and Border Protection (CBP) service, a bureau of the Department of Homeland Security. Because all of the 9/11 hijackers were noncitizens, in 2002 Congress chose to place many of the core immigration services, including border patrol and port inspections, under the auspices of the then newly created Department of Homeland Security (DHS).[3] DHS is also responsible for the initial processing of visa petitions originating

Figure 3.1 The Federal Immigration Bureaucracy

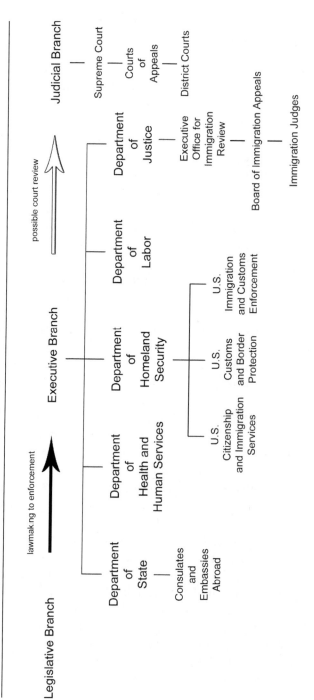

in the United States (for example, those filed by a stateside employer or relative) through its U.S. Citizenship and Immigration Services (USCIS) bureau. Homeland Security tracks those noncitizens who leave the United States voluntarily and also brings charges against those who have violated the terms of their stay and must be deported. The bureau responsible for prosecuting immigration cases is the U.S. Immigration and Customs Enforcement (ICE) service, which is staffed by trial attorneys for that specific purpose.[4]

You may recall from Chapter 1 that constitutional due process requires that at a minimum, the United States provide some safeguards to ensure a fair result before it deports a noncitizen, especially one who has lawfully been here for a long time. While the ICE trial attorneys of the DHS bring the charges, the Department of Justice grants the noncitizen a chance to have a hearing and review of the government's claims. Under the Executive Office for Immigration Review (EOIR), the Justice Department has set up a tribunal system that looks very much like a court, complete with immigration judges and a Board of Immigration Appeals (BIA). Unlike regular federal courts, however, the EOIR apparatus is part of the executive arm of the federal government and not a separate branch.[5] Because these are administrative, not federal, courts, many constitutional procedural safeguards do not apply. For example, whereas poor criminal defendants have the Sixth Amendment right to be represented by counsel for free,[6] indigent immigrants do not enjoy the right to free representation in immigration proceedings.[7]

Keeping this structure in mind should help you better comprehend the rules that govern the admission and expulsion of noncitizens, which I outline in the following section.

Basic Procedural Rules

Admission Procedures

Immigration scholar Steve Legomsky highlights the four basic procedural hurdles one must overcome in order to be admitted into the United States.[8] While a few of these hurdles may not apply to some noncitizens, they are all important to bear in mind.

First, as we learned in Chapter 2, certain noncitizens who are entering the United States to work must first obtain labor certification or approval of their labor condition applications. Failure to secure these approvals from the Department of Labor halts the immigration process for these applicants. Of course, if you qualify for a family-based visa or some other entry permit that does not require the Labor Department's approval, then you can move on to the next requirement. On March 28, 2005, the labor certification process entered the electronic age with the unveiling of an automated system known as Program Electronic Review Management (PERM). Under PERM, employers must comply with stringent advertising and recruitment requirements before they can electronically file for labor certification approval on a dedicated Department of Labor website.[9]

Second, some noncitizens must obtain approval of a visa petition filed in the United States. For instance, generally, a U.S. citizen must file an immediate relative visa petition for his foreign wife to be admitted; except in a few cases (where the wife is widowed or a battered spouse), she may not file the petition on her own. In contrast, a noncitizen hoping to visit Disneyland may apply directly for a tourist visa at the U.S. consulate in her home country without waiting for someone to file a petition on her behalf.

Immigrants must file one of two basic forms: for employer-sponsored petitions, the employer must use Form I-140; for family-sponsored petitions, the petitioning relative must use Form I-130. In addition to including detailed instructions on how to fill out the form, what processing fees apply, and what other documents you may need, the USCIS website (http://www.uscis.gov/portal/site/uscis) provides an overview of the process and then walks you through the current rules for these two petition types in the sections entitled "Immigration through a Family Member" and "Immigration through Employment," under the information regarding "Lawful Permanent Residence ('Green Card')." You may download many forms, including I-140 and I-130, as Adobe Acrobat (PDF) files from the website, or order them by mail.

Third, many noncitizens are required to physically obtain the visa from the U.S. consulate in their home country before traveling to America. While our tourist two paragraphs ago would have to comply with this requirement if she were Filipino, as we learned in Chapter 2, under the Visa Waiver Program, many citizens of western Europe may simply board a plane to Disneyland if they have a valid, machine-readable passport and do not plan to stay in the United States for more than ninety days.

Fourth, as mentioned earlier, the noncitizen must submit his or her entry documents to the U.S. Customs and Border Protection officer at the border for a final inspection before admission. The CBP officer has the authority to reexamine the noncitizen to make sure that none of the inadmissibility grounds we learned in Chapter 2 applies. If everything is in order, the officer will stamp the noncitizen's passport, indicating the date he or she arrived in and was admitted to the United States.

As was noted in the previous chapter, sometimes noncitizens run afoul of the terms of their stay. Although Homeland Security's ICE is responsible for determining which noncitizens it believes should be deported, if a person is stopped at the border, CBP would take him or her into custody. Let us now look at the basic procedural rules that govern the deportation or removal process.

Deportation Procedures

My goal here is to walk you through the different steps the government takes when it decides to seek a noncitizen's removal, from investigation of possible immigration violations, to basic removal procedures, to administrative appeals filed following removal.

Investigation and Prosecutorial Discretion

As we've learned, the U.S. Customs and Border Protection bureau and the U.S. Immigration and Customs Enforcement are currently charged with enforcing U.S. immigration laws. The CBP inspects noncitizens at the border, at fixed checkpoints near it, and occasionally, in other countries; Toronto, Canada, for instance, allows CBP officers to conduct immigration inspections of U.S.-bound passengers at the airport. ICE scrutinizes businesses suspected of hiring undocumented persons, coordinates with other federal and state police entities to deport criminal noncitizens, and investigates tips from informants.[10]

Pursuant to the political branches' plenary power to create and enforce immigration policy, the CBP and ICE enjoy a fair amount of prosecutorial discretion. Indeed, Congress has granted immigration authorities the power to "commence proceedings, adjudicate cases, or execute removal orders"[11] free from judicial review, which the Supreme Court upheld in *Reno v. American-Arab Anti-Discrimination Committee* (1999).[12] Following *Reno*, the Immigration Commissioner decided to publish a list of factors[13] that could warrant a favorable exercise of discretion leading to a decision *not* to prosecute, including LPR status, longtime residence in the United States, a relatively minor criminal offense, humanitarian concerns, lack of prior immigration violations, and so on. While this list is a useful guide to an ICE prosecutor deciding whether to commence proceedings, aggrieved noncitizens who believe they should not be deported do not have the right to invoke these factors in a lawsuit against the government.[14] Put another way, a deportee cannot successfully argue that he would have weighed the discretionary factors differently in deciding whether or not to seek his removal; the government places that discretion in the hands of the ICE prosecutor alone. Hence, a court will not second-guess a prosecutor's decision to seek deportation, but instead will see whether the prosecutor can successfully prove that the noncitizen should be removed.

Arrest, Detention, and Filing of the Notice to Appear

Part of the prosecutorial discretion immigration officers enjoy comes in the form of the power to arrest and detain noncitizens. While Congress has mandated pre-hearing arrest and detention in instances where a noncitizen's risk of flight or danger to others is high,[15] the Department of Homeland Security enjoys substantial leeway to simply serve the noncitizen instead with a "Notice to Appear," informing her of the immigration provisions the government believes she has violated,[16] or to agree to the noncitizen's release on bond. Most alleged deportees are not detained pending removal, and instead simply receive the Notice to Appear, which officially commences removal proceedings in the immigration court. As its name suggests, the Notice to Appear outlines the deportation charges that ICE believes warrant the noncitizen's removal so as to give her a chance to develop a response to the allegations.

Master Calendar Hearing

Shortly after the DHS files the Notice to Appear with the immigration court, a master calendar hearing is held during which the immigration judge (IJ) determines the scope of the charges being brought, whether the noncitizen intends to challenge deportation, and, if so, how both the government and the noncitizen might prepare for the hearing. Such preparation leading to the hearing itself gives meaning to the term *master calendar*: the IJ uses the hearing to set forth the calendar that will govern all pre-removal activity, including the taking of factual discovery and the filing of motions to change venue or suppress evidence, for instance. Remember that the IJ is an administrative law judge and not a regular federal court judge. As such, the IJ's job is as much about enforcing the law as it is about providing due process to the noncitizen. Unlike regular federal court judges, immigration judges are not constitutionally required to check abuses by the political branches; on the contrary, immigration judges help administer the rules promulgated by the political branches.

Removal Hearing

The removal hearing itself is held before an immigration judge who is part of the Executive Office for Immigration Review, the administrative wing of the Justice Department charged with providing due process to alleged deportees. As mentioned earlier, because this is not a trial but an administrative hearing, certain procedures are more informal and relaxed than one might expect, given the possible consequences to the noncitizen. For instance, instead of utilizing a live court reporter on site to produce it, the transcript of the hearing is derived from a tape recorder that the judge turns on at the beginning of the hearing. After the government establishes that the alleged deportee is a noncitizen, the noncitizen must respond by proving that he or she enjoys a valid immigration status. If the noncitizen is successful, the burden of proof then shifts to the ICE attorney to show that the noncitizen is deportable; the noncitizen then responds to these charges. If the judge finds the noncitizen deportable, the hearing may enter a second phase during which the noncitizen will raise any grounds for relief that may apply.[17] You may recall learning about these deportation grounds and the possible defenses in Chapter 2. After hearing all the evidence, the judge issues a reasoned decision, either orally from the bench or in writing, which is communicated to all parties.

Expedited Removal of Certain Noncitizens

One procedural innovation worth noting is the concept of expedited removal. Passed as part of Congress's anti-immigration initiative of 1996, expedited removal allows for the summary expulsion of arriving noncitizens who lack documents or have engaged in fraud.[18] Although seemingly a good idea, expedited removal creates a particularly difficult challenge to asylum seekers, who often arrive at the border without documents. While procedural safeguards are in place (including dedicated asylum officers charged with determining whether arrivals have a credible fear of persecution and limited review by an immigration judge), review by a regular federal court is virtually nonexistent.[19] Moreover, Congress gives the government the unreviewable discretion to extend expedited removal hearings to cover other situations, as it has done three times in recent years to certain noncitizens (1) convicted of the crime of entry without inspection; (2) who have arrived by sea without having been admitted or paroled, and who have not been continuously physically present in the United States for two years (adopted in 2002 in response to the large influx of Haitian boat people[20]); or (3) apprehended by an immigration officer for being present without admission within a certain distance from the border, unless they can prove continuous physical presence in the United States for the past fourteen days.[21]

Administrative Review:
BIA Appeals and Attorney General Certification
Recall that immigration courts are administrative ones: while they were created to provide due process to noncitizens, they are not meant to serve as a separate check on the executive branch's power (unlike regular federal courts), but instead are part of the executive branch's Department of Justice. Recall, too, that the Supreme Court implicitly supports this administrative structure through the plenary power precedent described in Chapter 1: when it comes to immigration policy, Congress enjoys virtually unlimited power to define the terms of a noncitizen's stay in the United States, whereas the president has similarly broad power to enforce congressional will through administrative agencies such as the U.S. Immigration and Customs Enforcement.

Pursuant to their plenary power, Congress and the president have created a fairly specific protocol for reviewing administrative decisions. Immigration scholar Richard Boswell notes that the easiest way to understand the appeals process is to "focus on the decision-making sequence—that is, who makes the initial decision, and then what body or bodies may review that determination (if it is reviewable)."[22] Deportation or removal orders by immigration judges may be appealed to the Board of Immigration Appeals (BIA). Recently and increasingly, immigration appeals have been decided by one BIA judge only rather than by the traditional three-judge panel,[23] leading to critics' charges that the gains in efficiency are outweighed by the lack of due process. Usually, the buck stops at the BIA in terms of administrative appeals. On occasion, however, the cabinet-level head, the Attorney General for the Justice Department, may decide to take jurisdiction over a case upon certification by the BIA or the DHS Secretary,[24] or on his or her own accord.[25]

It is important to remember that appeals to either the BIA or Attorney General do not provide the noncitizen with the opportunity to retry the case. Like other forms of appellate review, the BIA's or Attorney General's decision regarding removability and relief will be based solely on the factual record developed before the immigration judge. As Boswell reminds us, "conversations and other matters that do not appear in a written form and have not been submitted as part of the original application will not be considered on appeal. All requests for relief should be prepared as thoroughly as possible, as one cannot assume that there will be an opportunity to submit additional evidence. In fact, it is extremely rare that an applicant will have an opportunity to present new evidence in cases where he or she failed to do so initially."[26] Put differently, the noncitizen's best shot at presenting her side of the story is before the immigration judge who will get to listen to her live testimony, observe her demeanor, and discern her credibility. Because she will not be allowed to appear before the Board of Immigration Appeals, the noncitizen must ensure that she puts her best factual case before the immigration judge.

Naturalization Procedures

As we learned in Chapter 2, citizenship is the ultimate defense to a removal charge because only noncitizens may be deported; hence, many LPRs choose to naturalize to eliminate the threat of deportation. Immigration expert Allan Wernick warns, however, that applying for naturalization presents a risk: "When you apply for naturalization, you give the USCIS the opportunity to review your immigrant history. If you have committed an act that may make you removable, consult an immigration law expert before filing your application. Be especially careful if you have been convicted of a crime or if the USCIS may think that you obtained your permanent resident status improperly."[27] Removing immigrants who commit crime and fraud is a priority of the ICE, and so those whose backgrounds raise these red flags should seek immediate professional assistance. While some may regard a nonviolent DUI ("Driving Under the Influence" of drugs or alcohol, say) as a rather petty crime that could not possibly lead to deportation, ICE has decided that in some cases a DUI is a deportable offense. If you have a criminal record, no matter how explainable, seek expert help from a reliable immigration attorney before you decide to file for U.S. citizenship.

After meeting the requirements outlined in Chapter 2—LPR status for a period of years, good moral character, etc.—noncitizens interested in naturalization must file an "Application for Naturalization," USCIS Form N-400, which is available on the USCIS website (http://www.uscis.gov/portal/site/uscis) under "Immigration Forms." Along with filing the form, one must submit an application fee[28] and photographs, and have fingerprints taken. Wernick also suggests the following two tips when you file by mail, steps that should be taken anytime one submits paperwork to a government agency: (1) mail the application by certified mail with return receipt requested, and (2) keep a copy of all your documents and the return receipt in a safe place in case the original is lost or destroyed.[29]

A Special Case of Citizenship: Children

Chapter 2 briefly described two types of citizenship as the ultimate defense to a deportation charge: citizenship at birth, and naturalization. Because of the large number of mixed-immigration-status families in the United States and the prevalence of U.S. citizens adopting foreign-born orphans, it is worth taking a brief look at procedures regarding how children acquire citizenship.

Children may acquire U.S. citizenship in two ways: by being born in the United States or to a U.S. citizen abroad (birthright citizenship) or by becoming a citizen when a parent naturalizes or establishes adoptive custody (derivative citizenship).

Surprisingly, many noncitizens who grew up elsewhere do not realize that their birth in the United States or one of its territories[30] gives them U.S. citizenship. Wernick gives the example of a twenty-five-year-old man living in Haiti who falls in love with a U.S. citizen and wants to move to the United States to be with her. Having never considered himself an American, he and the U.S. authorities treat him as Haitian. His girlfriend, however, mentions in passing that the man had been born in New York City when his parents were studying there, but had never bothered to apply for citizenship. The man's mistake was that he did not have to apply for citizenship because his birth in New York automatically made him a U.S. citizen. In the hypothetical story, the girlfriend was able to obtain the man's U.S. birth certificate for him, which he then used to enter the United States the next day.[31]

Like birthright citizenship, a child born to U.S. citizen parents abroad automatically is a U.S. citizen from birth if *one* of the following three sets of conditions is met: (1) both parents were married U.S. citizens and one parent had resided in the United States; *or* (2) the parents were not married and either (a) one parent had been physically present in the United States for at least one year before the child's birth, or (b) the *father*[32] legitimated the child before his or her eighteenth birthday or agreed in writing to provide financial support to the child until he or she reaches eighteen; *or* (3) both parents were married, but only one was a U.S. citizen—in which case the U.S. citizen parent must have been physically present in the United States or one of its territories for five years before the child's birth, at least two of which were when the parent was over fourteen years old.[33]

Unlike birthright citizenship, derivative citizenship does not attach to a child at birth; rather, the child becomes a citizen upon the fulfillment of certain conditions. Unlike naturalization, however, derivative citizenship does not require that the child herself apply for citizenship; citizenship automatically ensues when the conditions are satisfied. The Child Citizenship Act of 2000 lists the four conditions under which a noncitizen child may become a U.S. citizen: (1) at least one parent is a U.S. citizen; (2) the child is less than eighteen years old; (3) the child resides in the United States in the citizen parent's custody; and (4) the child is an LPR.[34] Note that it does not matter in what order these four conditions are fulfilled; as soon as all are met, the noncitizen child automatically becomes a derivative citizen by virtue of the Child Citizenship Act. For example, a five-year-old foreign Ethiopian adoptee automatically becomes a U.S. citizen once her citizen parents residing in New York complete the adoption process under New York law by establishing their physical and legal custody.[35]

Wernick suggests that parents who would like to have specific proof of their child's U.S. citizenship should apply for a passport rather than a certificate of citizenship from the USCIS.[36] The passport is faster, cheaper, easier to obtain, and more useful, since you need a passport to travel abroad. For more on U.S. passports, see the State Department's website at http://travel.state.gov/passport/passport_1738.html.

The Role of the Federal Judiciary

The Supreme Court's deference to the political branches, and to administrative agencies that assist in enforcing the immigration law, limits the role that federal courts have in reviewing immigration court decisions. Richard Boswell notes that this deference to the political branches translates into a decided preference for administrative review over judicial oversight: "Courts may only review matters where the applicant has either exhausted available administrative remedies or where it would be futile to do so."[37] Note the two options here: a noncitizen facing deportation may choose to (1) exhaust his or her administrative remedies, or (2) seek court intervention only where proceeding administratively would be pointless. I will examine both these principles in more detail.

Exhaustion of remedies means that noncitizens wishing to challenge an immigration judge's ruling must proceed through the administrative agency's review process before seeking help from a federal judge. Specifically, this means following the administrative appeals path described earlier, from immigration judge, to the BIA, and sometimes to the Attorney General or Secretary of Homeland Security. To put it differently, noncitizens who bring arguments for the first time in federal court will be precluded from proceeding further; they must bring all their claims before the Executive Office for Immigration Review subagencies first. Those noncitizens who fail to follow this procedure will not receive their day in federal court, no matter how meritorious their claim. The reason behind this apparent stringency is to ensure that those with the most expertise on the nuances of immigration law and procedure—those administrative law judges and bureaucrats in the EOIR—have an adequate opportunity to address these issues fully before a generalist federal court reviews them.

Over time, this emphasis on and preference for administrative decisionmaking in immigration law have increased. In 1996 and 2005, Congress passed legislation designed to limit the number of cases that may be brought to federal court, making judicial review rarer.

We have encountered the 1996 acts before: the Antiterrorism and Effective Death Penalty Act (AEDPA) and the Illegal Immigration Reform and Immigrant Responsibility Act (IIRAIRA) were the sources of other anti-immigrant legislation, so it comes as no surprise that they were also the vehicles for the curtailment of judicial review.[38] These were followed by the passage of the REAL ID Act of 2005 close to ten years later, which limited judicial review even further.[39]

On occasion, however, the Supreme Court and Congress have recognized that working through the administrative process does not adequately secure noncitizens' rights. Prior to 1996, judicial review typically came in two forms: through habeas corpus relief and through the petition for review. Habeas corpus—which is Latin for "you may have the body"—refers to a federal district court action brought by someone who challenges her deportation proceeding; the "writ of habeas corpus," as the procedure is sometimes called, is guaranteed by the U.S. Constitution not to be suspended except in emergency situations.[40] In contrast, the petition for review is a creation of Congress by which noncitizens may ask a federal appeals court to review the BIA's decisions.[41]

Following the 1996 and 2005 amendments, Congress sharply limited these two avenues for review in order to shield certain types of immigration decisions from the judiciary's view. The REAL ID Act purports to restrict habeas corpus relief to district court actions where the claims concern constitutional allegations or questions of law only.[42] For example, in *Freeman v. Gonzales* (2006)[43] the court retained jurisdiction over the issue of whether an immediate relative beneficiary was entitled to immigrate despite the death of the petitioning spouse; the government argued that the petitioner's death automatically terminated the spouse's benefits and stripped the federal courts of jurisdiction over this case, but the court of appeals disagreed, ruling that the issue was a pure question of law. Similarly, direct petitions of review of final deportation orders have been relegated to the courts of appeals only,[44] and the act imposes a very high bar for the overturning of factual findings, requiring clear legal errors or abuses of discretion.[45]

Needless to say, the exact scope of judicial review is murky, but Congress's intent is clear: it wants to enable the executive branch to efficiently process deportations or exclusions without the federal courts second-guessing immigration authorities at every turn. From the noncitizen's perspective, however, having access to federal courts designed to check political power is an important democratic safety valve to ensure that all are treated fairly.

The Role of State and Local Law Enforcement Agencies

As was noted in Chapter 1, immigration law is the exclusive province of the federal government. Yet, the federal government does not have enough officers to investigate all possible immigration law violators; as of 2006, ICE had only about 6,000 criminal investigators for the entire nation.[46] This stark reality has led Congress to pass legislation allowing state and local governments to assist in enforcing immigration law, particularly with respect to apprehending criminal noncitizens. Specific laws permit states and local governments to (1) enter into written agreements with federal immigration authorities so their officers can receive training on how to investigate, apprehend, and detain immigration law violators;[47] (2) assist in an immigration emergency, such as an imminent mass influx of refugees;[48] and (3) arrest and detain undocumented persons who have reentered the United States after having previously been convicted of a felony and ordered deported.[49] In all these circumstances, enforcement is to be carried out by trained state and local police officers, not by other government employees generally, such as public school teachers or health care workers.

As of this writing, dozens of state and local entities have entered into formal written agreements with the federal government to enforce federal law: Alabama, Arizona, Florida, and the Los Angeles County Sheriff's Department were but the four earliest ones.[50] Many other municipalities around the country have passed their own anti-immigration laws without reference to specific congressional authorization; such laws are currently being challenged as illegal because they allegedly usurp the exclusive authority of Congress to regulate immigration law.[51] Two others—Alaska and Oregon—have taken the opposite tack by passing legislation forbidding the use of state and local resources to assist federal immigration enforcement efforts on the theory that this is the federal government's sole responsibility.[52] Some localities—such as New Haven, Connecticut, and New York City—have explicitly declared themselves "sanctuary" cities because they have chosen not to limit certain public benefits based on immigration status.

As Latino and Asian immigrants continue to populate once-majority-Caucasian towns around the country, we are likely to see states and local governments assert more control over their borders, particularly to the extent natives perceive immigrants, especially undocumented ones, to be a drain on their resources and a threat to their way of life. Undoubtedly, the federal courts will weigh in on whether such state and local infringement on a traditionally federal function without express congressional authorization is constitutional.

The Million-Dollar Question: Do I Need to Get an Attorney—or Not?

Here's the quick and dirty answer to the question of when to get an attorney: for most basic immigrant and nonimmigrant visa petitions (e.g., immediate relatives, tourist visas, etc.), you probably do not need an attorney; for more complex procedures having to do with deportation or detention (or if your case is complex—you have a criminal record and are applying to naturalize, for instance), you should consult one. Of course, part of the decision to consult an attorney depends on your own particular comfort level; some individuals may be willing to pay for the peace of mind of having an attorney do all of the paperwork for them, even if they could do it themselves.

If you decide to hire an attorney, here are two things you will want to remember: first, do not choose a lawyer solely because he promises that he will be able to expedite the government's processes for you. No private lawyer has control over that process, and to assure you otherwise should raise concerns. Instead, choose someone trustworthy, either by getting the name of an immigration law expert from someone you respect or by contacting the American Immigration Lawyers Association (AILA; see www.aila.org). Second, never rely on so-called paraprofessionals, who are not licensed to practice law, especially if they guarantee specific results at a reduced fee. While it is often tempting for foreign nationals on a limited budget to seek the assistance of paralegals or "notarios," many of whom may entice one by appealing to cultural or linguistic ties, the risk of wasting money with little benefit far outweighs the often empty promises of lower fees and expedited processing times.

As you may have gathered, much of the basics of immigration procedure regarding immigrant and nonimmigrant petitions—submitting forms and fees, meeting deadlines, gathering documentation—can be readily accomplished by the careful layperson who makes sure to keep copies of everything submitted, without the aid of an attorney. The pertinent information regarding forms and fees is clearly laid out on the USCIS's or State Department's Internet home pages—www .uscis.gov and www.state.gov, respectively—and in "how-to" guidebooks to immigration[53] available in one's local library.

Even if you are comfortable completing the paperwork yourself, a snag or delay may tempt you to seek a lawyer's help. Before you do that, keep in mind what we learned about the political nature of the immigration process. Because Congress has virtually unlimited power in enacting immigration law, federal senators and congresspersons are usually good sources of help should immigration petitions get bogged down in red tape and the process need to be expedited. Many congresspersons, especially from immigrant-rich states, have staffs dedicated to helping resolve constituents' immigration problems (as well as other related issues, like delays in processing social security cards). These staffers interact with counterparts within the immigration bureaucracy to address your concerns. Congresspersons find this staffing investment rewarding not just because they may be able to provide assistance, but because such assistance lifts their status in the eyes of the aided constituent. You can reach your representatives in the House at www.house.gov; for the Senate, consult www.senate.gov. Let us be clear, though: U.S. senators and representatives can help, but sometimes patience and persistence are one's only true allies in dealing with the inevitable delays that result from bureaucratic red tape. Our beleaguered immigration apparatus does not have sufficient staff to handle the volume of work it has before it; often, sympathizing with those behind the government desk, thanking them for their help, and getting their names so you can call upon them again go a long way toward making the process bearable for them and you.

Help with processing paperwork is one thing, but where one is being adjudicated in the system, however—say, as a person awaiting deportation—Congress is more reluctant to intervene and prefers to let the administrative process run its course. The reason for this hesitation makes sense when we think about the structure of immigration agencies. Remember that Congress saw fit to create this administrative structure to enforce immigration law, and so for legislators to intervene in a pending proceeding would evince a lack of trust in the very mechanism Congress established.

Should a person be ordered deported, the person can seek help from Congress by way of a private bill. Just as it sounds, the private bill is a special law enacted for the benefit of that single person. As you might imagine, private bills are rarely worth the effort, unless you have a particularly strong advocate in Congress who is sympathetic with the current reality that many deserving cases no longer receive judicial review; even if you find that one ally, remember that for a bill to become law, a substantial number of U.S. senators and representatives must support it, which appears less and less likely today, especially following the 1996 and 2005 anti-immigration amendments to the INA. During the 107th Congress in 2001–2002, for example, of the eighty-five private bills that were introduced, only one was enacted.[54]

Chapter 1 introduced two types of laws that affect noncitizens: immigration law—the law governing the entry and exit of noncitizens— and alienage law—all other laws affecting noncitizens. In Chapters 2 and 3, respectively, I examined the basic substantive and procedural laws affecting immigration. Next, in Chapter 4, I shift gears and focus on the alienage laws that affect noncitizens. In many ways, these alienage laws have much more of an impact on noncitizens' daily lives than the immigration laws that govern the terms of their stay in the United States.

Notes

1. See, e.g., Rick Lyman, "Census Shows Growth of Immigrants," *New York Times*, August 15, 2006, A1. See also Census Bureau, *United States Foreign Born Population*, available at http://www.census.gov/population/www/socdemo/foreign.html (last visited on Aug. 15, 2006); and Migration Policy Institute, *States Ranked by Percentage Change in the Foreign-Born Population: 1990, 2000, and 2005*, available at http://www.migration information.org/datahub/files/MPIDataHub_ACS_2006-PercentChange ForeignBorn.xls (last visited on Mar. 13, 2008).

2. Steve Legomsky has a chart that clearly outlines the organizational structure described in part here. See Stephen H. Legomsky, *Immigration and Refugee Law and Policy*, 4th ed. (New York: Foundation Press, 2005), 6.

3. Homeland Security Act of 2002, Pub. L. 107-296, 116 Stat. 2135 (Nov. 25, 2002). I have criticized the placement of immigration services under the Homeland Security department for perpetuating the stereotype that all immigrants are terrorists. See Victor C. Romero, "Race, Immigration, and the

Department of Homeland Security," *Journal of Legal Commentary* 19 (2004): 51.

4. You will note that the immigration services and enforcement functions are now housed in two separate bureaus of Homeland Security; prior to 2002, these functions were handled by one agency, the INS.

5. Specifically, the framers had in mind that the federal courts created under Article III would have a separate and distinct function from the Congress, described in Article I, or the president, described in Article II. As we learn in grade-school civics, the three branches were designed to promote democracy and prevent tyranny, in a system of checks and balances.

6. *Gideon v. Wainwright,* 372 U.S. 335 (1963).

7. Of course, they may pay for an attorney to represent them at their deportation hearing, if they so choose.

8. Legomsky, *Immigration and Refugee Law and Policy,* 451.

9. Austin T. Fragomen Jr. and Steven C. Bell, *Immigration Fundamentals: A Guide to Law and Practice,* 4th ed. (New York: Practicing Law Institute, 2004), 2-6 to 2-7.

10. Daniel Weissbrodt and Laura Danielson, *Immigration Law and Procedure,* 5th ed. (St. Paul, MN: Thomson West, 2005), 250.

11. INA § 242(g).

12. 525 U.S. 471 (1999).

13. For the complete list of factors, see Interpreter Releases, vol. 77, at 1673 (2000).

14. Weissbrodt and Danielson, *Immigration Law and Procedure,* 250.

15. Indeed, the Supreme Court upheld the mandatory detention provisions of 8 U.S.C. § 1226(c) in *Demore v. Kim,* 538 U.S. 510 (2003). In cases where detention is discretionary, the government generally sets a bond that the noncitizen can post to be able to be released pending the removal hearing. Should the noncitizen wish to challenge the DHS's bond decision, he or she may request a new bond hearing from the immigration judge. 8 CFR § 1003.19.

16. INA § 239(a)(1).

17. Recall that the substantive grounds for removal (e.g., moral turpitude crimes, aggravated felonies, etc.) and relief (e.g., cancellation of removal, asylum, etc.) were discussed in Chapter 2.

18. INA § 235(b)(1)(A)(i).

19. Under INA § 242(e)(2), a federal court may use habeas procedures to review a person's claim that (1) she is a citizen and therefore not subject to removal; or (2) she was not the person subject to the expedited removal order; or (3) she was a returning LPR and therefore should not have been subjected to expedited removal. Otherwise, all other merit claims are barred. Legomsky, *Immigration and Refugee Law and Policy,* 739.

20. For more on the Haitian refugees, see Brandt Goldstein, *Storming the Court* (New York: Scribner, 2005).

21. See Legomsky, *Immigration and Refugee Law and Policy*, 834.

22. Richard A. Boswell, *Essentials of Immigration Law* (Washington, D.C.: American Immigration Lawyers Association, 2006), 154.

23. Known as "streamlining," these summary affirmations of immigration judge decisions were promulgated via regulation in 1999 and 2002. See 8 CFR § 1003.1; 67 Fed. Reg. 54878 (2002); 64 Fed. Reg. 56135 (1999). See also Boswell, *Essentials of Immigration Law,* 161–162.

24. 8 CFR §§ 1003.1(h)(1)(ii) and (iii).

25. 8 CFR § 1003.1(h)(1)(i).

26. Boswell, *Essentials of Immigration Law,* 162. For more, see Fragomen and Bell, *Immigration Fundamentals,* ch. 8, at 8-1 to 8-62.

27. Allan Wernick, *U.S. Immigration and Citizenship: Your Complete Guide,* 4th ed. (Cincinnati: Emmis, 2004), 91.

28. Note that fee waivers are available for those who can prove they cannot afford it, unlike for most applications for permanent residence. Ibid., 127.

29. Ibid., 126.

30. By "territories," I mean Puerto Rico, the U.S. Virgin Islands, Guam, and the Mariana Islands. A person born in American Samoa or Swain's Island is a U.S. national who is eligible to carry a U.S. passport. Wernick, *U.S. Immigration and Citizenship,* 130; Weissbrodt and Danielson, *Immigration Law and Procedure,* 408–411.

31. Wernick, *U.S. Immigration and Citizenship,* 130–131.

32. The Supreme Court upheld the different conditions applicable to mothers and fathers in *Nguyen v. INS,* 533 U.S. 53 (2001).

33. Ibid., 131; INA §§ 301 and 309. These sections also outline rules for persons born during different time periods. See, e.g., INA § 301(h) (rule that applies to person born outside the United States before noon Eastern Standard Time on May 24, 1934).

34. Child Citizenship Act of 2000, Pub. L. 106-395, 114 Stat. 1631 (Oct. 30, 2000).

35. The law used to require that the parents apply for naturalization after having completed the state adoption paperwork, and many would fail to do so, leading to the deportation of many noncitizen children upon reaching adulthood. The Child Citizenship Act corrected that problem by making citizenship automatic upon the completion of the state adoption paperwork. See Victor C. Romero, "The Child Citizenship Act and the Family Reunification Act: Valuing the Citizen Child as Well as the Citizen Parent," 55 *Florida Law Review* 589 (2003). Wernick reminds us that a separate derivative citizenship rule exists for children who turned eighteen years old before February 27, 2001, the effective date of the Child Citizenship Act. See Wernick, *U.S. Immigration and Citizenship,* 134.

36. Wernick, *U.S. Immigration and Citizenship,* 134. One must file USCIS Form N-600 for the certificate. Relatedly, children born abroad who

do not qualify for either birthright or derivative citizenship may have N-600K forms filed on their behalf. For details, see the USCIS website at http://www.uscis.gov/graphics/formsfee/forms/n-600k.htm.

37. Boswell, *Essentials of Immigration Law,* 154.

38. See AEDPA, Pub L. No. 104-132, 110 Stat. 214 (1996); and IIRAIRA, Pub. L. No. 104-208, 110 Stat. 3009 (1996).

39. REAL ID Act of 2005, Division B of Pub. L. 109113, 119 Stat. 231 (May 11, 2005).

40. U.S. Constitution, Art. III, § 3.

41. See Act of September 26, 1961, Pub. L. No. 87-301, § 5, 75 Stat. 650, 651.

42. The amended judicial review section of the INA reads: "Nothing . . . which limits or eliminates judicial review, shall be construed as precluding review of constitutional claims or questions of law raised upon a petition for review. . . ." INA § 242(a)(2)(D).

43. 444 F.3d 1031 (9th Cir. 2006).

44. INA §§ 242(a)(2)(A)(i) and 242(a)(2)(D).

45. Boswell, *Essentials of Immigration Law,* 167.

46. See Eric Lipton, "Boston Tests System Connecting Fingerprints to Records of Immigration Violations," *New York Times,* September 9, 2006 (noting that "Immigration and Customs Enforcement has a squad of only about 6,000 criminal investigators").

47. 8 U.S.C. § 1357(g).

48. 8 U.S.C. § 1103(a)(8).

49. 8 U.S.C. § 1252c.

50. Lisa M. Seghetti, Stephen R. Viña, and Karma Ester, "Enforcing Immigration Law: The Role of State and Local Law Enforcement," *Congressional Research Service (CRS) Report for Congress,* January 27, 2006, at CRS-17; see also U.S. ICE, Delegation of Immigration Authority Section 287(g) Immigration and Nationality Act, available at http://www.ice .gov/pi/news/factsheets/070906factsheet287gprogover.htm (last visited on Mar. 13, 2008).

51. See, e.g., Michael Powell and Michelle Garcia, "Pa. City Puts Illegal Immigrants on Notice," *Washington Post,* August 22, 2006, A03 (describing state and local anti-immigration laws around the country).

52. Seghetti et al., "Enforcing Immigration Law," CRS-25. Note that Oregon's law does permit state and local police to exchange information with federal authorities to verify that a criminal arrestee is a noncitizen.

53. Allan Wernick's volume referenced here, *U.S. Immigration and Citizenship,* is a particularly user-friendly one.

54. Legomsky, *Immigration and Refugee Law and Policy,* 614.

4

Alienage Laws and Contemporary Immigrant Issues Post-9/11

In this chapter I explore contemporary civil rights issues that may affect foreign nationals aside and apart from their immigration woes. To put it differently, this chapter switches from the earlier focus on immigration law to alienage law: to those federal, state, and local government laws that affect the day-to-day life of noncitizens living in the United States. Irrespective of Congress's plenary power over immigration law, discussed in Chapter 1, other federal, state, and local laws may provide noncitizens in the United States substantial protection (or, in the case of more recent draconian local laws, may attempt to effectively deport them from the area). For example, while undocumented migrants live under the threat of deportation, if they should work, their employers are required to pay them the prevailing wage for their labor. The list of issues I explore here is by no means exhaustive but is meant to provide applications of the general rule that outside immigration law, noncitizens may sometimes find protection under favorable federal, state, and local alienage laws that may not immediately occur to them.

This chapter is divided into two parts: the first surveys federal, state, and local laws that define the rights of noncitizens outside immigration law. The alienage laws that will be examined include those relating to accessing public benefits like education and welfare, obtaining employment, and securing housing. The second part focuses on other contemporary immigrant rights issues that have arisen post-9/11 in the shadow of the government's so-called war on terror.

Treatment in this section will be brief but broad, covering a range of related topics from border security to identification cards to noncitizen military service; it aims to provide the reader with an overview of how the war on terror has driven much of our current immigration-related policy while only occasionally striking the proper balance between maintaining national security and safeguarding freedom.

Alienage Law Basics: Federal, State, and Local Law Protections for Noncitizens Outside Immigration Law

By no means exhaustive, this discussion of alienage law will focus on the most common legal issues that confront noncitizens outside the realm of immigration policy.

Access to Public Benefits
Education
Primary and Secondary School (K–12). Regardless of their immigration status, all noncitizen residents have the right to attend free public elementary and secondary school education in any state that offers this to its U.S. citizen residents. So long as a state offers free public education, all undocumented children are able to attend for free as well. In *Plyler v. Doe* (1992),[1] Texas enacted a law that denied undocumented migrant children free public education, arguing that because such children were not here lawfully, state taxpayers should not be required to subsidize their education. A bare 5-to-4 majority of the Supreme Court struck down the Texas law because it violated the Fourteenth Amendment's command that no state deny any person equal protection of the laws. Justice Brennan's opinion noted that undocumented children were not to be blamed for their status; it was their parents, not they, who had made the conscious decision to come to this country. Moreover, Brennan worried that the Texas law would create a permanent underclass of illiterate immigrant children. Thus, because of the *Plyler* decision, all noncitizen children—documented or not—may enroll in the local public schools in which they reside. The schools are not allowed to ask their immigration status on school forms, nor may they charge these students a tuition fee.

One significant caveat is worth noting here: because many municipal governments have recently passed laws designed to deter undocumented migration, some local school districts might be tempted to ask their students for proof of their lawful immigration status. Remember that *Plyler v. Doe* gives these students and their families the right to refuse to answer that question. Unless the Supreme Court specifically overturns *Plyler*, undocumented children and their advocates have cause to challenge overzealous school districts that may unwittingly seek to trample upon protected constitutional rights; a simple letter to your school district officials and solicitor citing *Plyler* might be a place to start.

Postsecondary Education (College and University). Unlike in the lower grades, publicly subsidized postsecondary education is generally *not* available to undocumented residents, except as allowed under state law. *Plyler* applied to K–12 schools only, and while some[2] have advocated its extension to college and university settings, the Court has not done so. As of this writing, ten states—California, Illinois, Kansas, Nebraska, New Mexico, New York, Oklahoma, Texas, Utah, and Washington—have laws providing for in-state tuition regardless of a person's federal immigration status.[3]

In significant part, these state laws measure eligibility for lower in-state tuition rates based on whether one graduated from a state high school after having attended for a specific number of years. California's 2002 statute,[4] for example, allows undocumented students the opportunity to attend schools in the state university and community college system without having to pay out-of-state tuition rates if they (1) attended a California high school for three years; (2) graduated from a California high school (or the equivalent thereof); (3) were registered students at a California college or university beginning in the fall of 2001–2002; and (4) sign an affidavit affirming their application for legalization of their immigration status or their intent to file for legalization at the earliest opportunity. Under the law, undocumented students' immigration status will be kept confidential and will not be disclosed to the federal immigration authorities. Many of the other state laws follow a similar pattern.

While this positive trend at the state level has been welcomed by many advocates, these laws cannot provide a pathway to legal immigration status, which we have learned can only be accomplished by Congress. A 2003 Urban Institute report estimated that 65,000 undocumented minors who have lived in the United States for at least five years graduate from American high schools each year.[5] Accordingly, many immigrant rights groups have been pushing for the federal DREAM (Development, Relief, and Education for Alien Minors) Act, a bipartisan effort that could help several hundred thousand children legalize their status. The Migration Policy Institute opined that, had the bill passed in 2006, some 279,000 high school graduates would have been eligible for college enrollment or the U.S. military.[6]

Because of the recent wrangling in Congress over general legalization for undocumented migrants, it is unclear whether growing support for the DREAM Act may be stalled. Advocates remain cautiously optimistic, however, that because the focus of this legislation is on helping children who are not responsible for their immigration status, keeping this issue on the front burner will ultimately lead to the act's passage.

English Language Instruction and Policy. Education policymakers have long debated how best to help noncitizens assimilate through the medium of instruction. To put it simply, one side believes noncitizen children should be schooled in the English language only, regardless of when and how they came to this country. Others decry that approach as naïve, arguing that creating lifelong learning requires effective communication, which is best accomplished by instruction in students' native languages. While it is not solely immigration related (recall the national debate regarding Ebonics), the issue of whether to fund more than "English only" instruction will continue to grow as the nation's immigrant population swells.

The key for many emerging immigrant-rich communities is to study the example of states and localities that have successfully adopted and implemented legislation designed to best serve the interests of migrant students. For instance, North Dakota, which is not a traditionally immigrant-rich state, passed a 2007 law providing extra compensation to school districts that serve "new immigrant English language learners," supporting the districts financially while allowing them leeway to explore how best to serve this student population.[7]

Health and Welfare

Today, almost all social welfare benefit programs, even those at the state and local government levels, involve federal participation. And because the modern welfare state has become increasingly federalized over time, alienage restrictions on both state and federal benefits enjoy the more relaxed scrutiny the Court affords Congress.[8] Although a blessing when Congress acts generously, alienage provisions in welfare laws usually have been restrictive, especially since 1996.

Perhaps better known as a "welfare-to-work" initiative of the Clinton administration, the federal Personal Responsibility and Work Opportunity Reconciliation ("Welfare") Act of 1996 also aimed to reduce the number of noncitizens dependent on welfare by limiting all federal, state, and local welfare benefits to "qualified aliens" only.[9] "Federal public benefits" include the following types of aid either provided by a federal agency or by using appropriated U.S. funds: (1) grants, contracts, loans, professional or commercial licenses; (2) retirement, welfare, health, disability, housing, postsecondary education, food assistance, unemployment; and (3) any other similar benefits to an individual, household, or family.[10] The phrase *qualified aliens* refers to a specific list of eligible noncitizens lawfully present in the United States on a more or less permanent basis, whether as lawful permanent residents (LPRs), refugees, parolees, or political beneficiaries (e.g., Cubans and Haitians); undocumented migrants, temporary visa holders, and overstays do not qualify.[11] Despite this restrictive definition, undocumented persons and others are still eligible for limited government assistance such as emergency medical care, temporary noncash emergency disaster relief, and public health assistance for immunizable and communicable diseases.[12]

For "qualified" noncitizens, the Welfare Act's most notable restriction was the creation of a five-year bar on any federal means-tested public benefits for those arriving on or after August 22, 1996, the act's effective date. As its name suggests, "means-tested" benefits are provided to those who fall below a certain level of income and therefore do not have the means to support themselves. The adoption of the five-year bar was likely tied to the usual residence period required to naturalize, effectively making means-tested public benefits open to U.S. citizens only. In addition, Congress found significant fraud in the acquisition of supplemental security income (SSI) and food stamp benefits, prompting it to place a permanent bar on most noncitizens' eligibility for these until they naturalize or have worked at least forty qualifying quarters; certain asylees, refugees, veterans, and those on active duty in the armed forces are exempt from these restrictions.[13]

The House Ways and Means Committee Report summarized these restrictions as being consistent with the nation's historical approach: "[The Welfare Act] returns American policy on welfare for noncitizens to its roots by barring most noncitizens who arrive in the future from receiving welfare benefits."[14] Because an immigrant's likelihood of becoming a public charge is a ground for inadmissibility (as was discussed in Chapter 2), it makes sense that Congress has limited the availability of welfare benefits to fewer noncitizens; even so, Congress realized that these restrictions must be balanced against the need to provide reasonable support to those who, through no fault of their own, require essential government assistance to deal with unforeseen emergencies.

States administering federal benefits now receive block grants with which to design and implement their own welfare programs. Immigration experts Austin Fragomen and Steven Bell characterize states as having been "generous" overall by developing, for instance, their own food stamp replacement programs to benefit elderly, minor, and disabled immigrants; eighteen states have developed such procedures.[15] Furthermore, all states have chosen to allow unqualified immigrants—including undocumented ones—to continue to benefit from WIC, the food supplement program for women, infants, and children, and almost all have chosen to continue immigrant eligibility for TANF (Temporary Assistance for Needy Families), Medicaid, and Social Services block grant benefits. As with in-state college tuition benefits, a few states have set aside state TANF and Medicaid funds for new immigrants barred by the federal five-year bar on means-tested benefits; Fragomen and Bell describe California's program as being particularly generous.[16]

Employment Issues

As mentioned earlier, noncitizens who wish to work in the United States must be granted authorization by the U.S. Citizenship and Immigration Services (USCIS), usually per approval by the Labor Department, in order to protect U.S. citizens and LPRs in the workforce. Consequently, all employers are required to verify the employment eligibility of all prospective employees, whether citizen or noncitizen, by having them complete a USCIS Form I-9, Employment Eligibility Verification. Employees do not include independent contractors, "casual domestic hires" (the person hired to clean houses once a week, for instance), and workers employed prior to November 6, 1986 (the effective date of the Immigration Reform and Control Act—IRCA—of 1986, which established these eligibility rules).[17]

Immigration expert Allan Wernick advises employers to copy the front and back of the I-9 forms (also available online at the USCIS website) and then distribute these to employees, directing them to the reverse side,[18] which lists documents they can present to establish their identity and employment eligibility. Specifically, a noncitizen has to present either one document that establishes both his or her identity and employment eligibility or a separate document for each. For instance, an LPR need only present her "green card" to show that she is eligible to work; a nonimmigrant may wish to show his school photo ID card and an employment authorization document from the Department of Homeland Security (DHS) to qualify. Wernick advises eligible noncitizens who have been asked by employers to produce additional or different documentation to call the Office of Special Counsel for Immigration Related Unfair Employment Practices (800-255-7688; http://www.usdoj.gov/crt/osc/) for advice.[19] To expedite claims, the Office of Special Counsel (OSC) has created a telephone intervention program where OSC staff members try to resolve issues brought by employees informally with employers, so as to avoid investigatory delays and litigation costs.

The employers' failure to verify employment eligibility and keep adequate records of the same subjects them to civil and, if sufficiently egregious, criminal penalties. Because of the recent debate over undocumented immigration and mounting pressure from both Congress and the public, Immigration and Customs Enforcement (ICE) has been particularly keen on more strictly enforcing employer sanctions, including by way of workplace raids. State and local governments have also passed laws punishing employers for knowingly hiring undocumented persons, although their constitutionality is currently being considered by the courts.[20]

If you are an employer seeking current guidance on how to verify the employment eligibility of prospective workers, consult the USCIS website's "Employer Information" section under its "Services & Benefits" tab. Although initially authorized as part of the Illegal Immigration Reform and Immigrant Responsibility Act in 1996, a recent alternative to the I-9 paper-based process described previously is USCIS's "E-Verify" procedure, a voluntary online program that allows employers to verify employee eligibility of newly hired workers against DHS database information, which includes biometric identifiers (see www.dhs.gov/E-Verify). Note that E-Verify cannot be used to screen prospective employees but is intended to be used to verify eligibility once the employment decision has been made. Some states have sought to create employer sanctions for failure to comply with the federal I-9 process, and one—Arizona—even requires employers to use the voluntary E-Verify program. In response, the National Immigration Law Center (NILC) has criticized this approach, citing the government's own findings that the E-Verify database contains numerous errors.[21]

Fearful that the employment eligibility verification laws would lead to discrimination against "foreign-looking" employees, Congress also passed a law punishing any employer that discriminates on an illegal basis, including national origin and race; discriminating against undocumented persons, however, is not illegal because they are not authorized to work.[22] Nonetheless, if an employer hires an undocumented person and then either pays less than the minimum wage or not at all, the worker is entitled to back pay under the Fair Labor Standards Act, even if not entitled to be rehired.[23] For example, in a federal court proceeding for recovery of these monies under the act, the worker's attorneys should request that their client's immigration status be kept sealed because it is irrelevant to receiving compensation for work rendered.

If you have immigrated to the United States, you should apply for a Social Security card, which provides proof of your eligibility for retirement benefits through the federal Social Security Administration (SSA) (www.ssa.gov). Increasingly, employers receive "Employer Correction Request," or so-called no-match, letters from the SSA, stating that the Social Security numbers reported on an I-9 form do not match the names in their records. Note that these letters do not imply that a noncitizen employee is ineligible to work or is subject to deportation due to fraud; simple errors such as misspellings, using one's married name, or inverting two numbers may explain the discrepancy. While the SSA has no enforcement power and does not share these letters with the immigration authorities, employees should correct these errors as soon as practicable.[24]

Housing Issues—Property Ownership

Because state law generally governs the ownership of land, noncitizens must comply with the laws of the state when they plan to purchase real property. Daniel Weissbrodt and Laura Danielson note that all fifty states allow LPRs who have applied for citizenship the opportunity to own property.[25] Unfortunately, state property laws are not uniform with respect to other classes of noncitizens, and many states regulate the ability of nonresident and absent noncitizens to purchase property.[26] Given the lack of uniform treatment of noncitizens under these diverse state laws, their constitutionality is an open question, although with so many other pressing legal issues surrounding immigration, it is not one that courts will likely address anytime soon.

As with employment issues, the federal government requires that landlords and sellers not discriminate on the basis of race or national origin. The Department of Housing and Urban Development enforces the federal Fair Housing Act, providing assistance at http://www.hud.gov/complaints/housediscrim.cfm, or 800-669-9777. Just as state property laws do not treat noncitizens equally, the Fair Housing Act does not make noncitizenship a protected class; consequently, some state and local governments have sought to punish landlords who knowingly rent to undocumented persons. Like the anti-immigrant local employment laws, these are also being challenged in courts because they interfere with the federal immigration system.[27]

Contemporary Immigrant Issues in Post-9/11 America: Balancing Security and Freedom

Although U.S. immigration policy has long been concerned with national security, securing our borders became the foremost priority after the tragic terrorist attacks of September 11, 2001. Government officials felt particular pressure to explain how so many of the 9/11 hijackers—all noncitizens—could escape detection. In response, Congress created the Department of Homeland Security and placed the existing immigration apparatus under its purview. As we move further away in time from September 11, U.S. immigration focus has appeared to shift away from "immigrants as terrorists" to "immigrants as criminals." While the overwhelming majority of foreign-born persons in the United States are neither, and while studies conclusively show that native-born persons are more likely to engage in crime than immigrants,[28] many of the contemporary immigration issues discussed today appear to focus on the immigrant as criminal, from the terrorist to the border-crosser. This chapter concludes with a sampling of these issues, as they are likely to be part of any discussion about immigrant rights and immigration policy for years to come.

Border Security

Much of the debate surrounding comprehensive immigration reform in 2006 and 2007 focused on balancing border security with undocumented migrant amnesty. Balking at amnesty and compromising on security, Congress passed and President George W. Bush signed the Secure Fence Act of 2006 on October 26, 2006.[29] This law famously authorized the creation of 700 miles of new fence along the southern border with Mexico, despite an acknowledgement that there were no funds to pay for this project. The act pits anti-immigrant zealots like the Minutemen against individuals and local communities who object to the fence being built on their property. Whereas advocates like Congressman Duncan Hunter hail the two-tier fence as a primary reason why border crossings in the San Diego area decreased dramatically from 1992 to 2004,[30] detractors like immigration experts Douglas Massey and Demetrios Papademetriou argue that enhanced border security has the unintended consequence of preventing temporary migrants from returning home.[31] Tighter border security has also forced more migrants and smugglers to cross into the United States at more dangerous points, including across the Sonoran Desert in southern Arizona, which has seen a record number of deaths in recent years.[32]

Notwithstanding these negative effects, the government appears undeterred. At the end of 2007, the DHS reported that it intends to "enable construction of roughly 670 miles of fencing by the end of December 2008," although it did not specify how much of this would be new construction.[33] In the meantime, the Government Accountability Office released its September 2007 study of unstaffed areas on both the Canadian and Mexican borders, finding that its investigators were freely able to cross into the United States at certain locations.[34] Such evidence has prompted Massey to argue that instead of wasting money on a border fence, we should invest in Mexican economic development, better ports and transportation systems, and a more robust U.S. guest worker program.[35] Such observations have apparently fallen on deaf ears; more recent federal activity in 2008 included talk of a "virtual" border fence and the introduction of numerous border security bills in Congress.

Identification Cards

Post-9/11 pundits and scholars alike raised concern over the hijackers' use of state driver's licenses to board the planes that fateful day. The REAL ID Act of 2005[36] was Congress's response: it mandates that federal agencies will not accept state-issued identification cards, including driver's licenses, unless they conform to certain security specifications promulgated by the Department of Homeland Security. Like the border issue, uniform identity cards have stirred controversy among states and civil rights groups alike. The American Civil Liberties Union contends that the REAL ID Act not only will be costly to implement in terms of dollars and time but also will not make us more secure because determined terrorists will find ways to obtain counterfeit identification cards anyway.[37] Substantial opposition by many states caused the DHS to provide over $35 million in grant funding in December 2007, in anticipation of the implementation deadline of May 2008.[38]

Aside from concerns about terrorism, others value REAL ID because it would deter undocumented persons from obtaining driver's licenses, limiting their ability to illegally hold jobs here. Detractors counter that licensing undocumented persons both enhances road safety and provides a mechanism for tracking their presence; former New York governor Eliot Spitzer was the foremost proponent of this idea when he pushed forth such a plan for the state, only to back off in November 2007 due to fierce constituent opposition.[39] On a smaller scale, New Haven, Connecticut, successfully created the Elm City Resident Card, which provides identification to all city residents—including undocumented persons—with the ability to access city services, from libraries to swimming pools to parking meters; residents are expected to be able to use it to open bank accounts as well. Funded by a private grant and approved by the city council in June 2007, the card is the first of its kind in the country.[40] Like New Haven, other like-minded communities have experimented at other times with the SIGO card (a debit card issued by MasterCard) and the matrícula consular (a Mexican-government issued ID) as means of providing undocumented persons access to local community services. Given the controversy raging over the REAL ID Act, time will tell whether the federal government will try to curb local efforts to provide support to undocumented migrants in their communities.

Noncitizens in the U.S. Military

Any person who serves honorably in the military for a period aggregating one year is eligible to apply for naturalization.[41] In addition, all LPRs from the age of eighteen to twenty-six are required to register for the draft via the Military Service Act; nonimmigrants are exempt.[42]

With the so-called war on terror showing no signs of abatement, some criticize the armed services' targeted recruitment of Latino youths, using the promise of immigration benefits as the hook. While the National Defense Authorization Act of 2006 focuses on the enlistment of citizens and LPRs, it also specifically provides for the enlistment of others if deemed vital to the national interest.[43] News reports describe military recruiters approaching Latino youths with promises of citizenship for themselves or relatives who have been deported: "Do you have anybody in your family that needs a green card, needs papers?"[44] Counterrecruitment groups charge that the armed services fail to adequately inform applicants of the significant risks that attend combat duty, the only jobs available to unskilled high school graduates.[45]

Relatedly, some have criticized the yet-to-pass DREAM Act's provisions that allow for a pathway to citizenship for undocumented youth via military service. As discussed earlier, the DREAM Act would allow undocumented high school graduates the opportunity to attend college and create a pathway for their naturalization. While applauding the education provisions that open college doors for the undocumented, critics worry that most youth will choose the military over college.[46]

Unaccompanied Immigrant Children

The National Center for Refugee and Immigrant Children estimates that over 7,000 children are stopped at the border by the immigration authorities annually.[47] These children are often undocumented, unaccompanied, and fleeing persecution or abuse; their cases are handled by the Department of Health and Human Services rather than by either USCIS or ICE. Still, their youth makes these children particularly vulnerable and in need of guidance to ensure that they receive the services necessary to navigate the immigration bureaucracy. Though advocacy groups and volunteer attorneys work to address the issue, others argue that our resources should be used to service Americans rather than noncitizens. In response to news that the National Center for Refugee and Immigrant Children was to open a North Carolina branch, Gordon Baum of the Council of Conservative Citizens remarked that "[the government] ought to worry about monitoring and decreasing the flow. It's an injustice to the working people of North Carolina."[48]

Studying immigration law is like studying politics or religion: there are no easy answers, and proponents on either side of an issue tend to feel passionately about their position. I hope that this short book has helped you gain a better understanding of the larger themes in U.S. immigration and immigrant rights policy, as well as some of the specific intricacies of the law, some of which may seem peculiar to the casual observer. Yet, if there is a single message I wish to convey, it is that the everyday laws governing immigrants are exceedingly complex. I therefore invite you to consider the resources in Chapter 5 for further guidance.

Notes

1. 457 U.S. 202 (1982).

2. See, e.g., Victor C. Romero, "Postsecondary School Education Benefits for Undocumented Immigrants: Promises and Pitfalls," 27 *North Carolina Journal of International Law and Commercial Regulation* 393 (2002).

3. See Dawn Konet, "Unauthorized Youths and Higher Education: The Ongoing Debate," September 2007, at Migration Policy Institute website, http://www.migrationinformation.org/Feature/display.cfm?id=642 (last visited on Dec. 28, 2007); and Ann Morse, "In-State Tuition and Unauthorized Immigrant Students," July 26, 2006, at National Conference of State Legislatures website, http://www.ncsl.org/programs/immig/immig_InState Tuition0706.htm (last visited on Dec. 28, 2007).

4. See California Education Code § 68130.5: "Notwithstanding any other provision of law: (a) A student, other than a nonimmigrant alien within the meaning of paragraph (15) of subsection (a) of Section 1101 of Title 8 of the

United States Code, who meets all of the following requirements shall be exempt from paying nonresident tuition at the California State University and the California Community Colleges:

(1) High school attendance in California for three or more years.
(2) Graduation from a California high school or attainment of the equivalent thereof.
(3) Registration as an entering student at, or current enrollment at, an accredited institution of higher education in California not earlier than the fall semester or quarter of the 2001–2002 academic year.
(4) In the case of a person without lawful immigration status, the filing of an affidavit with the institution of higher education stating that the student has filed an application to legalize his or her immigration status, or will file an application as soon as he or she is eligible to do so.
(b) A student exempt from nonresident tuition under this section may be reported by a community college district as a full-time equivalent student for apportionment purposes.
(c) The Board of Governors of the California Community Colleges and the Trustees of the California State University shall prescribe rules and regulations for the implementation of this section.
(d) Student information obtained in the implementation of this section is confidential."

5. Jeffrey S. Passel, "Further Demographic Information Relating to the DREAM Act," the Urban Institute, October 21, 2003, available at http://www.nilc.org/immlawpolicy/DREAM/DREAM_Demographics.pdf (last visited on July 3, 2007).

6. Jeanne Batalova and Michael Fix, "New Estimates of Unauthorized Youth Eligible for Legal Status Under the DREAM Act," Migration Policy Institute, October 2006, available at http://www.gcir.org/new/reports/pdfs/Backgrounder_Dream_Act.pdf (last visited on July 3, 2007).

7. See North Dakota SB 2200, signed into law on May 3, 2007, as reported in the NCSL Immigrant Policy Project, 2007 Enacted State Legislation Related to Immigrants and Immigration, November 29, 2007, available at http://www.ncsl.org/programs/immig/2007Immigration831.htm (last visited on Dec. 28, 2007).

8. Austin T. Fragomen Jr. and Steven C. Bell, *Immigration Fundamentals: A Guide to Law and Practice*, 4th ed. (New York: Practicing Law Institute, 2004), 9-5.

9. See Pub. L. No. 104-193, 110 Stat. 2105 (Aug. 22, 1996), as amended by the Illegal Immigration Reform and Immigrant Responsibility Act of 1996, Pub. L. No. 104-208, 110 Stat. 3009 (Sept. 30, 1996).

10. Fragomen and Bell, *Immigration Fundamentals*, 9-6.

11. Ibid.

12. Ibid. Aside from receiving these emergency benefits, those who do not fall under one of the enumerated "qualified alien" categories but are otherwise "lawfully present" may receive federal retirement, disability, and auxiliary benefits under Title II, as well as Medicare Part B. Ibid., 9-7.

13. Ibid., 9-10; see also Daniel Weissbrodt and Laura Danielson, *Immigration Law and Procedure,* 5th ed. (St. Paul, MN: Thomson West, 2005), 530.

14. Committee on Ways and Means, U.S. House of Representatives, "Summary of Welfare Reforms Made by Public Law 104-193: The Personal Responsibility and Work Opportunity Reconciliation Act and Associated Legislation," November 6, 1996, available at http://www.access.gpo.gov/congress/wm015.pdf (last visited on July 3, 2007).

15. Fragomen and Bell, *Immigration Fundamentals,* 9-12. These states are California, New York, Texas, Florida, Illinois, New Jersey, Massachusetts, Maryland, Colorado, Washington, Minnesota, Rhode Island, Ohio, Connecticut, Missouri, Maine, Wisconsin, and Nebraska.

16. Ibid., 9-12. See also Michael Fix and Jeffrey Passel, *The Scope and Impact of Welfare Reform's Immigrant Provisions* (Washington, D.C.: Urban Institute, 2002), available at http://www.eric.ed.gov/ERICWebPortal/custom/portlets/recordDetails/detailmini.jsp?_nfpb=true&_&ERICExt Search_SearchValue_0=ED462496&ERICExtSearch_SearchType_0=no& accno=ED462496 (last visited on Dec. 28, 2007).

17. See INA § 274A. For the specific federal regulations implementing this law, see 8 CFR § 274a.2 (verification of employment eligibility).

18. Allan Wernick, *U.S. Immigration and Citizenship: Your Complete Guide,* 4th ed. (Cincinnati: Emmis, 2004), 218.

19. Ibid., 231.

20. See, e.g., *Lozano v. City of Hazleton,* Case 3:06-cv-01586-JMM (July 26, 2007), available at http://www.aclu.org/pdfs/immigrants/hazleton_decision.pdf (last visited on Dec. 28, 2007) (declaring unconstitutional Hazleton, Pennsylvania's law proscribing the hiring of undocumented persons).

21. National Immigration Law Center, "Why States and Localities Should Not Require Employers to Participate in the Basic Pilot/E-Verify Program," January 15, 2008, available at http://www.nilc.org/immsemplymnt/ircaempverif/basicpilot_stateslocalities_2008-01-15.pdf (last visited on Mar. 13, 2008).

22. INA § 274B(a)(1). These employer antidiscrimination provisions apply to employers of four or more employees but are not intended to displace more generally applicable federal antidiscrimination laws regarding employment. INA § 274B(a)(2).

23. See *Hoffman Plastic Compound, Inc. v. National Labor Relations Board,* 535 U.S. 137 (2002).

24. In 2007 the Department of Homeland Security was temporarily enjoined by a federal court from sending guidance letters to employers accompanying the "no match" letters; although these guidance letters were intended to weed out undocumented workers, immigrant advocates feared they would lead to the firing of authorized employees, given the likelihood of minor errors in the SSA database. See Migration Information Source, "Top 10 Migration Issues of 2007," 3 (available at http://www.migration information.org/issue_dec07.cfm), published by the Migration Policy Institute (Washington, D.C.) (last visited on May 28, 2008).

25. Weissbrodt and Danielson, *Immigration Law and Procedure,* 548.

26. Fragomen and Bell, *Immigration Fundamentals,* 9-15.

27. See, e.g., *Lozano v. City of Hazleton,* Case 3:06-cv-01586-JMM (July 26, 2007), available at http://www.aclu.org/pdfs/immigrants/hazleton_ decision.pdf (last visited on Dec. 28, 2007) (declaring unconstitutional Hazleton, Pennsylvania's law proscribing the tenancy of undocumented persons). More recently, federal district courts in Arizona, Oklahoma, and Missouri have *upheld* similar anti-immigrant laws.

28. "Numerous studies by independent researchers and government commissions over the past 100 years repeatedly and consistently have found that immigrants are *less* likely to commit crimes or be behind bars than the native-born." Immigration Policy Center, "Immigrants and Crime: Are They Connected?" December 2007, accessed from http://www.ailf.org.

29. Pub. L. No. 109-367, 120 Stat. 2638 (2006).

30. "As local congressman and presidential candidate Duncan Hunter notes, 'The success of the San Diego Border Fence demonstrates the overall effectiveness of the double-layered approach and the importance of extending this infrastructure across the southern land border.'" "De-fence, Defence," December 20, 2007, available at http://money.cnn.com/news/ newsfeeds/articles/newstex/IBD-0001-21797675.htm (last visited on Dec. 29, 2007).

31. Mireya Navarro, "Traditional Round Trip for Workers Is Becoming a One-Way Migration North," *New York Times,* December 21, 2006.

32. "As they increasingly avoid heavily patrolled urban areas, they cross with little or no knowledge of the desert, whose heat, insects, wildlife and rugged terrain make it some of the most inhospitable terrain on the planet." Randal C. Archibold, "At the U.S. Border, the Desert Takes a Rising Toll," *New York Times,* September 15, 2007.

33. Press Release, "DHS Moves Forward on Border Fencing and Technology Improvements," December 7, 2007, available at http://www.dhs .gov/xnews/releases/pr_1197058374853.shtm (last visited on Dec. 29, 2007).

34. U.S. Government Accountability Office, "Border Security: Security Vulnerabilities at Unmanned and Unmonitored U.S. Border Locations," September 27, 2007.

35. Tyche Hendricks, "Study: Price for Border Fence up to $49 Billion," *San Francisco Chronicle,* January 8, 2007, B-1 (available at http://sfgate .com/cgi-bin/article.cgi?f=/c/a/2007/01/08/BAG6RNEJJG1.DTL).

36. Division B of Pub. L. 109-13, 119 Stat. 231 (May 11, 2005).

37. See the ACLU's "Real Nightmare" website at http://www.real nightmare.org/.

38. Press Release, Department of Homeland Security, "DHS Releases REAL ID Grant Guidance," available at http://www.dhs.gov/xnews/ releases/pr_1197580232137.shtm (last visited on Dec. 29, 2007).

39. "New York Governor Spitzer Abandons Driver's Licenses for Illegals Plan," FOXNews.com, November 14, 2007, available at http://www .foxnews.com/story/0,2933,311544,00.html (last visited on Dec. 29, 2007).

40. Melissa Bailey, "City ID Plan Approved," *New Haven Independent,* June 5, 2007, available at http://newhavenindependent.org/archives/2007/ 06/city_id_plan_ap.php (last visited on Dec. 29, 2007).

41. INA § 328(a).

42. 50 U.S.C. App. § 453.

43. § 542(b)(1) and (2), Pub. L. 109-163, 119 Stat. 323, January 6, 2006.

44. Deborah Davis, "Yo Soy el Army: If You're an Immigrant, at Least Uncle Sam Wants You," *Metroactive,* September 19, 2007, available at http://www.metroactive.com/metro/09.19.07/news-0738.html (last visited on Dec. 31, 2007).

45. Ibid.

46. Daniel González, "A Military Route to Citizenship," *Arizona Republic,* September 17, 2007, available at http://www.azcentral.com/arizona republic/news/articles/0917dreamwar0917.html (last visited on Dec. 31, 2007).

47. Visit their website at http://www.refugees.org/article.aspx?id=1260 &subm=75&area=Participate.

48. Nitisha Desai, "New N.C. Center to Aid Undocumented Children," *Daily Tar Heel,* November 1, 2006, available at http://media.www.daily tarheel.com/media/storage/paper885/news/2006/11/01/StateNational/ New-N.c.Center.To.Aid.Undocumented.Children-2413849.shtml (last visited on Dec. 31, 2007).

5

Selected Bibliography and Resource Guide

Introductory Note About Accessing Online Sources

Throughout this book I reference immigration forms and other information readily available on the Internet because most federal government agencies now put all of this material on the web. Agencies find this method more convenient and cost-effective, especially in keeping their information up-to-date. Therefore, I do not recommend relying on print sources for government materials, as they may not be current. However, if you do not have ready access to a computer, please go to your local library because it likely will have a free public-access terminal. The reference staff can give you instructions on how to use the computer. If your community library does not have this information, you should consider going to a U.S. Federal Government Depository Library, which has to provide public access to federal information as part of the depository program, including access to online government forms.

For more general information regarding federal government agencies, consider these two references: (1) *Guide to U.S. Government Publications*, published by Gale biennially, lists U.S. government agency publications; and (2) *United States Government Manual*, published annually by the Government Printing Office, describes federal agencies, their key officials, programs, and contact information. The *Government Manual* is also available online at http://www.gpoaccess.gov/gmanual/index.html.

Selected Bibliography

It would be impossible to catalog the many excellent resources regarding U.S. immigration and policy that exist. However, the following six books proved particularly useful in writing this one:

T. Alexander Aleinikoff, David A. Martin, and Hiroshi Motomura,
    *Immigration and Nationality Laws of the United States: Selected
    Statutes, Regulations and Forms* (St. Paul, MN: Thomson West,
    2007).
Richard Boswell, *Essentials of Immigration Law* (Washington, D.C.:
    American Immigration Lawyers Association, 2006).
Austin T. Fragomen Jr. and Steven C. Bell, *Immigration Funda-
    mentals: A Guide to Law and Practice*, 4th ed. (New York:
    Practicing Law Institute, 2004).
Stephen H. Legomsky, *Immigration and Refugee Law and Policy*, 4th
    ed. (New York: Foundation Press, 2005; also a 2007 supplement).
Daniel Weissbrodt and Laura Danielson, *Immigration Law and
    Procedure*, 5th ed. (St. Paul, MN: Thomson West, 2005).
Allan Wernick, *U.S. Immigration and Citizenship: Your Complete
    Guide*, 4th ed. (Cincinnati: Emmis, 2004).

The rest of this bibliography refers to various Internet and print
resources for accessing information on immigration and immigrants,
some scholarly and some practical. The most recent and reliable material regarding current laws will likely be found on government
websites, and so I have listed those resources first.

Government
U.S. Department of Justice
http://www.usdoj.gov

Agencies Under the Department of Justice
Civil Rights Division (CRD)
http://www.usdoj.gov/crt/crt-home.html

Executive Office for Immigration Review (EOIR)
http://www.usdoj.gov/eoir

Department of Homeland Security (DHS)
http://www.dhs.gov

Homeland Security Components
U.S. Citizenship and Immigration Services (USCIS)
http://www.uscis.gov

U.S. Customs and Border Protection (CBP)
http://cbp.gov

U.S. Immigration and Customs Enforcement (ICE)
http://www.ice.gov/index.htm

U.S. Department of Labor
http://www.dol.gov

Hiring foreign labor: http://www.dol.gov/dol/topic/hiring/foreign
.htm

U.S. Department of State
http://www.state.gov

Diplomatic list: http://www.state.gov/documents/organization/
73346.pdf

Foreign Consular Offices in the United States: http://www.state.gov/
documents/organization/71117.pdf

U.S. Department of Health and Human Services
http://www.hhs.gov

Information on medical examination of aliens: http://www.cdc.gov/
ncidod/dq/health.htm

Nonprofit Organizations, Forums, Blogs, and Resources
American Bar Association (ABA) Commission on Immigration
http://www.abanet.org/publicserv/immigration/home.html

The ABA Commission on Immigration focuses on fair treatment and
due process rights of immigrants. The website contains resources including publications and a directory of immigration legal providers.

American Civil Liberties Union (ACLU) Immigrants' Rights
http://www.aclu.org/immigrants/index.html

ACLU Immigrants' Rights advocates for immigrant, refugee, and noncitizen rights by challenging the constitutionality of laws that negatively impact these groups.

American Immigration Law Foundation (AILF)
http://www.ailf.org

AILF has four core program areas that serve to educate the public on immigration policy and advocate for immigrant rights: the Legal Action Center, Immigration Policy Center, Public Education Program, and Exchange Visitor Program.

American Immigration Lawyers Association (AILA)
http://www.aila.org

AILA is a national association composed of attorneys and law professors in the immigration field. The website contains useful resources for lawyers and immigrants alike.

American-Arab Anti-Discrimination Committee
http://www.adc.org

The American-Arab Anti-Discrimination Committee is a civil rights organization that offers legal counseling on discrimination and defamation and serves through impact litigation on immigration, discrimination, and civil rights.

Amnesty International
http://www.amnesty.org

Amnesty International campaigns to fight human rights violations throughout the world.

Asian American Justice Center (AAJC)
http://www.advancingequality.org

The AAJC serves Asian Americans by advancing human and civil rights through advocacy, public policy, public education, and litigation.

Asian Law Caucus
http://www.asianlawcaucus.org

The Asian Law Caucus serves low-income Asian Pacific American communities through representation in immigration and civil rights issues.

Asian Pacific American Legal Center (APALC) of
Southern California
http://www.apalc.org

APALC services include civil rights advocacy, legal services, and policy analyses affecting immigrants, specifically in Asian American communities.

Capital Area Immigrants' Rights (CAIR) Coalition
http://www.caircoalition.org/

CAIR provides training and education, information, and legal support services to individuals and organizations that represent immigrants.

Catholic Legal Immigration Network, Inc. (CLINIC)
http://www.cliniclegal.org

CLINIC serves indigent immigrants through legal and nonlegal support services and serves the Catholic Church in the United States through religious immigration services.

Center for Human Rights and Constitutional Law
http://centerforhumanrights.org

The Center for Human Rights and Constitutional Law advances civil, constitutional, and human rights of immigrants and refugees through litigation and legislative advocacy.

Coalition for Human Immigrant Rights of Los Angeles (CHIRLA)
http://www.chirla.org

CHIRLA seeks to advance the rights of immigrant groups through community education, policy advocacy, and community organizing.

Colombian American Service Association (CASA)
http://www.casa-usa.org

CASA assists immigrants through legal counseling, representation, family support, employment, and referrals.

Emerald Isle Immigration Center of New York
http://www.eiic.org

The Emerald Isle Immigration Center of New York provides services including immigration, citizenship, and employment referrals to Irish immigrants in New York City.

The Florence Project
http://www.firrp.org

The Florence Project provides free legal services to detainees of the Immigration and Customs Enforcement in Florence and Eloy, Arizona. Nationally, it is a resource and training center for legal providers to detainees.

Global Rights
http://www.globalrights.org

Global Rights is an international organization that advocates for human rights.

Human Rights First
http://www.humanrightsfirst.org

Human Rights First is a nonprofit organization that advocates for human rights of refugees, victims of crimes against humanity, and victims of discrimination.

Human Rights Initiative (HRI)
http://www.hrionline.org

HRI provides legal and social services to victims of human rights abuses in their homelands.

Human Rights Watch
http://www.hrw.org

Human Rights Watch is an independent nonprofit organization that serves to protect human rights around the world. The website has much useful information, including reports specific to country.

Immigrant Legal Resource Center (ILRC)
http://www.ilrc.org

The ILRC is a national resource center promoting immigrant rights through education and advocacy.

Immigration Equality
http://immigrationequality.org

Immigration Equality advocates for lesbian, gay, bisexual, transgender, and HIV-positive individuals and their equal rights under immigration laws.

Immigration History Research Center, University of Minnesota
http://www.ihrc.umn.edu

This research center maintains and preserves a large collection of research materials on immigration that serves as an intellectual resource for scholars, ethnic communities, organizations, educators, and researchers.

ImmigrationProf Blog
http://lawprofessors.typepad.com/immigration/

Edited by leading immigration law scholars, this blog contains useful scholarly and popular information on events and people in the world of migration.

Irish Immigration Center
http://www.iicenter.org

The Irish Immigration Center serves the Irish immigrant community by providing legal advice, information advocacy, and support on immigration, employment, citizenship, housing, and social services.

League of United Latin American Citizens (LULAC)
http://www.lulac.org

LULAC advances educational attainment, economic conditions, political influence, and health and civil rights of Hispanic Americans.

Lutheran Immigration and Refugee Service (LIRS)
http://www.lirs.org

LIRS provides legal and social services to refugees and immigrants, advocates for immigrant and refugee rights, and provides training to other groups that provide similar services.

Mexican American Legal Defense and Educational
Fund (MALDEF)
http://www.maldef.org

MALDEF serves the Latino community through litigation, advocacy, and educational outreach.

National Coalition for Haitian Rights
http://www.nchr.org

The National Coalition for Haitian Rights advances Haitian rights in the United States and Haiti.

National Council of La Raza (NCLR)
http://www.nclr.org

The NCLR is a civil rights and advocacy organization serving Hispanic Americans, specifically in five areas: assets/investments, civil rights/immigration, education, employment and economic status, and health.

National Immigrant Justice Center
http://www.immigrantjustice.org

The National Immigrant Justice Center provides comprehensive legal immigration services and reform advocacy and litigation.

National Immigration Forum
http://www.immigrationforum.org

The National Immigration Forum advocates for immigration policies that welcome immigrants.

National Immigration Law Center (NILC)
http://www.nilc.org

NILC provides information and analyses on proposed legislation and regulations affecting immigrant groups and advocates and litigates to protect immigrant rights.

National Immigration Project of the National Lawyers Guild, Inc.
http://www.nationalimmigrationproject.org

The National Immigration Project provides legal support particularly for immigrants facing deportation and incarceration.

National Network for Immigrant and Refugee Rights (NNIRR)
http://www.nnirr.org/index.html

The NNIRR is a forum for activist groups that facilitates information-sharing to help immigrants and refugees.

Refugee Law Center
http://www.refugeelawcenter.org/

The Refugee Law Center provides legal representation, research, educational initiatives, and policy development serving the victims of human rights abuses.

Refugees International
http://refugeesinternational.org

Refugees International serves refugees and displaced persons through advocacy.

The Rights Working Group (RWG)
http://www.rightsworkinggroup.org

The Rights Working Group is composed of national and regional organizations committed to ensuring due process and equal protection for all, especially noncitizens, in the United States. The RWG Steering Committee includes organizations ranging from the ACLU and AILA to the New Jersey Immigration Policy Network and the Tennessee Immigrant and Refugee Rights Coalition.

Southeast Asia Resource Action Center (SEARAC)
http://www.searac.org

SEARAC seeks to further the interests of Cambodian, Laotian, and Vietnamese Americans through advocacy and information-sharing, leadership development, and coalition building.

Women's Commission for Refugee Women and Children
http://www.womenscommission.org

The Women's Commission is an expert resource that advocates for refugee women and children.

Books
Asylum and Refugees
Broken Spirits: The Treatment of Traumatized Asylum Seekers, Refugees, War and Torture Victims
Editors: John P. Wilson and Boris Drožek
Brunner-Routledge (2004)

Compilation of articles focusing on psychological treatment of traumatized asylees and refugees.

Desperate Crossings: Seeking Refuge in America
Authors: Norman L. Zucker and Naomi Flink Zucker
M. E. Sharpe, Inc. (1996)

Discusses U.S. refugee policy, specifically pertaining to Cuba, Haiti, and Central America.

Refugees in America in the 1990s: A Reference Handbook
Editor: David W. Haines
Greenwood Press (1996)

Focuses on the largest refugee groups in the United States.

Detention and Removal
American Gulag: Inside U.S. Immigration Prisons
Author: Mark Dow
Regents of the University of California (2004)

Provides a background on the practice of detaining noncitizens. Also contains accounts and realities of those detained indefinitely in immigration detention centers.

Detained: Immigration Laws and the Expanding INS Jail Complex
Author: Michael Welch
Temple University Press (2002)

Explores the "moral panic" and its effects on 1996 immigration laws, and provides information on enforcement of immigration laws and detention operations.

Other People's Blood: U.S. Immigration Prisons in the Reagan Decade
Author: Robert S. Kahn
Westview Press (1996)

Talks about the abuse experiences in prisons of refugee and asylum seekers who were denied protection by the United States during the 1980s.

Gender, Sexuality, and Immigration

Entry Denied: Controlling Sexuality at the Border
Author: Eithne Luibhéid
Regents of the University of Minnesota (2002)

Explores how women have been excluded in U.S. immigration because of their sexuality, which was seen as threatening to national security during the late nineteenth century and early twentieth century.

Gender and U.S. Immigration: Contemporary Trends
Editor: Pierrette Hondagneu-Sotelo
Regents of the University of California (2003)

An anthology of essays on gender and U.S. immigration in the context of employment, ethnic identities, citizenship, and so on. Some chapters were previously published in various sources.

Passing the Lines: Sexuality and Immigration
Editors: Brad Epps, Keja Valens, and Bill Johnson Gonzalez
Harvard University Press (2005)

Explores the interaction between sexuality and sexual orientation, and U.S. immigration, specifically focusing on immigration from Latin America and the Caribbean.

The Qualities of a Citizen: Women, Immigration, and Citizenship, 1870–1965
Author: Martha Gradner
Princeton University Press (2005)

Discusses immigration laws as applied to women from the 1870s to the 1960s.

Guides to U.S. Immigration
The Complete Success Guide for the Immigrant Life:
How to Survive, How to Thrive, How to Be Fully Alive
Author: Monette Adeva Maglaya
PDI Books (2004)

Provides useful information for new immigrants, such as legal immigrant statuses, basics for newcomers, family matters, education and career, money matters, entrepreneurship, and more.

Easy Immigration: A Guide for Success
Author: Nejib Adem
AuthorHouse (2006)

A practical manual for immigrants seeking citizenship.

Fiancé and Marriage Visas: A Couple's Guide to U.S. Immigration
Author: Ilona Bray
Nolo (2005)

A guide to immigrating to the United States through marriage.

Hello USA! Everyday Living for International
Residents and Visitors
Author: Judy Priven
Hello! America, Inc. (2002)

Contains useful information about the United States for newcomers, foreign residents, and visitors.

How to Get a Green Card: All the Forms and Step-by-Step
Instructions You Need to Call the United States "Home"
Authors: Ilona Bray and Loida Nicolas Lewis
Nolo (2005)

A step-by-step guide for those eligible to apply for a green card.

How to Immigrate to the U.S.: Live, Work, and Retire—the Easy Way
Author: Adam Starchild
Books for Business (2001)

Discusses the various types of visas, ways to apply for permanent resident status, grounds for exclusion, and citizenship.

Immigration Made Simple: An Easy-to-Read Guide to the U.S. Immigration Process
Authors: Barbara Brooks Kimmel and Alan M. Lubiner
Next Decade, Inc. (2006)

Provides helpful basic information on the various statuses, laws, and procedures in the U.S. immigration system.

Immigration the Easy Way
Author: Susan N. Burgess
Barron's Educational Series, Inc. (2003)

A guide to U.S. entry and immigration.

Living and Working in America: The Complete Guide to Studying, Working, or Living in the U.S.A.
Author: Steve Mills
How to Books Ltd. (2004)

Provides information on living conditions in the United States. Helpful for first-time visitors, especially those interested in living temporarily in the United States.

U.S. Immigration and Citizenship Q&A
Authors: Debbie M. Schell, Richard E. Schell, and Kurt A. Wagner
Sphinx Publishing (2003)

Using a question-and-answer format, this book provides information on immigrating to the United States organized by what the immigrant wants to do as opposed to categorizing the migrant by specific visas.

U.S. Immigration Step by Step
Author: Edwin T. Gania
Sphinx Publishing (2004)

Self-help book on U.S. immigration. Includes various visas, forms, and other practical information for immigrants and petitioners.

Win the Green Card Lottery! The Complete Do-It-Yourself Guide to the USA Diversity Visa Lottery Plus Other Ways to Get a Green Card, Lottery Service Reviews, and More!
Authors: Marybeth Rael and J. Stephen Wilson
Editor: James T. Daly
Creative Networks (2005)

Provides information on how to enter the Diversity Visa lottery. Updates and e-books available at http://www.mygreencard.com/index.php

Immigration History
Americans in Waiting: The Lost Story of Immigration and Citizenship in the United States
Author: Hiroshi Motomura
Oxford University Press (2006)

Examines the history of immigration in the United States and the various issues that arose during the formative years of U.S. immigration and alienage laws.

At America's Gates: Chinese Exclusion During the Exclusion Era, 1882–1943
Author: Erika Lee
University of North Carolina Press (2003)

Traces the story of Chinese immigration and the exclusion laws.

Deportation Nation: Outsiders in American History
Author: Daniel Kanstroom
Harvard University Press (2007)

Comprehensively examines U.S. deportation policies throughout history, arguing that removal has long been a staple of U.S. immigration law.

Guarding the Golden Door: American Immigration Policy and Immigrants Since 1882

Author: Roger Daniels
Hill and Wang (2004)

Discusses U.S. immigration policy from 1882 to the twenty-first century.

The Huddled Masses Myth
Author: Kevin R. Johnson
Temple University Press (2003)

Argues that much of U.S. immigration history reflects the racism and xenophobia present in contemporaneous domestic laws.

Immigration: From the Founding of Virginia to the Closing of Ellis Island (Eyewitness History Series)
Author: Dennis Wepman
Facts on File, Inc. (2001)

Covers immigration history from a firsthand perspective and provides photographs, documents, maps, and key figures in immigration.

A Nation by Design: Immigration Policy in the Fashioning of America
Author: Aristide R. Zolberg
Russell Sage Foundation Books (2006)

Traces American immigration policy through history and discusses the social and political factors that contributed to the formative development of U.S. immigration policy.

Opening the Floodgates: Why America Needs to Rethink Its Borders and Immigration Laws
Author: Kevin Johnson
New York University Press (2007)

Argues for a more liberal U.S. immigration policy that restricts movement only in cases of true threats to society.

Other Immigrants: The Global Origins of the American People
Author: David M. Reimers
New York University Press (2005)

Provides an account of non-European immigration in American history.

Immigration Policy: Society, Economics, and Politics

Alienated: Immigrant Rights, the Constitution, and Equality in America
Author: Victor C. Romero
New York University Press (2005)

Explores the constitutional tension between equal treatment and citizenship discrimination inherent in America's treatment of noncitizens.

Beyond Citizenship: American Identity After Globalization
Author: Peter J. Spiro
Oxford University Press (2007)

Argues that modern-day loyalties are increasingly transnational and determined by things other than U.S. citizenship.

The Chosen Shore: Stories of Immigrants
Author: Ellen Alexander Conley
Regents of the University of California (2004)

Features personal accounts of various immigrant Americans.

The Citizen and the Alien: Dilemmas of Contemporary Membership
Author: Linda Bosniak
Princeton University Press (2006)

Examines the tension created by immigration policies and alienage laws that often send contradictory messages of inclusion and exclusion.

A Companion to American Immigration
Editor: Reed Ueda
Blackwell Publishing (2006)

An anthology of essays about U.S. immigration throughout history.

Contemporary World Issues: U.S. Immigration
Author: Michael LeMay
ABC-CLIO, Inc. (2004)

Provides an overview of U.S. immigration laws, policies, and procedures. Contains key acts, cases, and issues. Also contains a chronology of immigration policies by era, influential people in U.S. immigration, and a directory of agencies and organizations.

Deporting Our Souls
Author: Bill Ong Hing
Cambridge University Press (2006)

Discusses major immigration policy areas such as undocumented workers, national security, and integration of immigrants in American society.

Enemy Aliens
Author: David Cole
The New Press (2003)

Examines the post-9/11 treatment of noncitizens accused of terrorist activity in light of U.S. immigration history and policy.

Fences and Neighbors: The Political Geography of Immigration Control
Author: Jeanette Money
Cornell University Press (1999)

Explores why some countries are more welcoming of immigrants than others.

A Framework for Immigration: Applications to Asians in the United States
Author: Uma Segal
Columbia University Press (2002)

Focuses on Asian immigrants, their reasons for migrating, and the issues they face in American society.

Human Traffic: Sex, Slaves, and Immigration
Author: Craig McGill
Vision Paperbacks (2004)

Gives accounts of various undocumented immigrants through interviews and case studies.

Immigration and Crime: Race, Ethnicity, and Violence
Editors: Ramiro Martinez Jr. and Abel Valenzuela Jr.
New York University Press (2006)

An anthology of essays exploring crimes related to immigration, ultimately arguing that stereotypes linking immigrants to crimes are unsubstantiated.

Immigration and the Politics of American Sovereignty, 1890–1990
Author: Cheryl Shanks
University of Michigan Press (2001)

Discusses U.S. immigration policy from a political perspective.

Immigration Policy and the Welfare System
Editors: Tito Boeri, Gordon Hanson, and Barry McCormick
Oxford University Press (2002)

Examines immigration and welfare politics in both the United States and European Union from a theoretical and empirical perspective.

Lock Out: Why America Keeps Getting Immigration Wrong When Our Prosperity Depends on Getting It Right
Author: Michele Wucker
PublicAffairs (2006)

Points out past mistakes in U.S. immigration policy and makes a primarily economic argument for America's need for immigrants.

The New Americans: How the Melting Pot Can Work Again
Author: Michael Barone
Regnery Publishing (2006)

Rejects multiculturalism but argues for allowing undocumented immigrants to stay and learn American values and achieve the American dream.

Probationary Americans: Contemporary Immigration Policies and the Shaping of Asian American Communities

Authors: Edward J. W. Park and John S. W. Park
Taylor and Francis Group (2005)

Discusses immigration policies in the context of racial groups, arguing that U.S. immigration policies focus on race and class.

*Reinventing the Melting Pot: The New Immigrants and
What It Means to Be American*
Editor: Tamar Jacoby
Basic Books (2004)

Discusses assimilation of new immigrants in American society.

*Strangers Among Us: How Latino Immigration
Is Transforming America*
Author: Robert Suro
Alfred A. Knopf (1998)

Analyzes the effects of Latin immigration in American society.

*To Be an American: Cultural Pluralism and the
Rhetoric of Assimilation*
Author: Bill Ong Hing
New York University Press (1997)

Discusses economic and social effects of immigrants, particularly focusing on immigrant jobs, costs, and interethnic divides.

To Be an Immigrant
Author: Kay Deaux
Russell Sage Foundation (2006)

Focuses on the immigrant experience with a social psychology perspective. Topics include policies, attitudes toward immigration, and ethnic identity.

Unwelcome Strangers
Author: David M. Reimers
Columbia University Press (1998)

Traces the various policy arguments from pre–World War II to the late 1990s. Provides perspectives from restrictionists, assimilationists, and others.

We Are All Suspects Now: Untold Stories from Immigrant Communities After 9/11
Author: Tram Nguyen
Beacon Press (2005)

Explores the immigrant communities targeted as suspects, and the unjust treatment by the government that they have been subjected to since 9/11.

Why Does Immigration Divide America? Public Finance and Political Opposition to Open Borders
Author: Gordon H. Hanson
Institute for International Economics (2005)

A study of the economic debate that divides America on immigration issues.

Undocumented Immigrants
At Issue: What Rights Should Illegal Immigrants Have?
Editor: Lori Newman
Greenhaven Press/Thomson Gale (2006)

An anthology of articles debating whether undocumented migrants should have specific rights. Arguments from both sides are presented.

Impossible Subjects: Illegal Aliens and the Making of Modern America
Author: Mae M. Ngai
Princeton University Press (2005)

Argues that the restrictionist immigration policies of the early twentieth century led to the current undocumented immigration problem of today.

Operation Gatekeeper: The Rise of the "Illegal Alien" and the Remaking of the U.S.-Mexico Border
Author: Joseph Nevins
Routledge (2001)

Examines immigration policies along the U.S. border with Mexico from both a historical and a contemporary perspective.

Shadowed Lives: Undocumented Immigrants in American Society
Author: Leo R. Chavez
Harcourt Brace College Publishers (2nd ed., 1998)

Provides an in-depth anthropological study of undocumented workers in Southern California, particularly in San Diego County.

News Sources

The Immigrant Portal
Available online at http://www.ilw.com

Provides news, classifieds, a lawyer directory, and other useful information on immigration law.

Migration News
Available online at http://migration.ucdavis.edu/mn/about_mn.php

"Migration News summarizes and analyzes the most important immigration and integration developments of the preceding quarter. Topics are grouped by region: North America, Europe, Asia, and Other."

Law Journals

African Law Journal
Publisher: Africa Law Institute

Asian American Law Journal
Publisher: Boalt Hall School of Law, University of California, Berkeley

Asian Pacific American Law Journal
Publisher: University of California, Los Angeles, School of Law

Asian-Pacific Law and Policy Journal
Publisher: University of Hawaii, William S. Richardson School of Law

Berkeley La Raza Law Journal
Publisher: Boalt Hall School of Law,
University of California, Berkeley

Chicano-Latino Law Review
Publisher: University of California, Los Angeles,
School of Law

Columbia Human Rights Law Review
Publisher: Columbia University School of Law

Georgetown Immigration Law Journal
Publisher: Georgetown University Law Center

Harvard Human Rights Journal
Publisher: Harvard Law School

International Journal of Refugee Law
Publisher: Oxford University Press

Northwestern University Journal of International Human Rights
Publisher: Northwestern University School of Law

Treatises and Manuals and Other Sources for Lawyers
Asylum Case Law Sourcebook
Produced in cooperation with David A. Martin
Publisher: Thomson/West

Bender's Immigration and Nationality Act Service
Publisher: Matthew Bender and Company, Inc.

Bender's Immigration Bulletin
Publisher: Matthew Bender and Company, Inc.
Note that Bender also has a daily edition of its bulletin online at
http://bibdaily.com/.

Bender's Immigration Regulations Service
Publisher: Matthew Bender and Company, Inc.

Business Immigration Law: Strategies for Employing
Foreign Nationals
Authors: Rodney A. Malpert and Amanda Petersen
Publisher: ALM Properties, Inc., Law Journal Press, a Division of
American Lawyer Media, Inc.

The Criminal Lawyer's Guide to Immigration Law:
Questions and Answers
Author: Robert James McWhirter
Publisher: American Bar Association

Gordon, Mailman, and Yale-Loehr Immigration
Law and Procedure
Authors: Charles Gordon, Stanley Mailman, and Stephen Yale-Loehr
Publisher: Matthew Bender and Company, Inc.

Guide to Homeland Security
Publisher: Thomson/West

Guidebook for Foreign Labor Certification
Authors: members of the Academy of Business Immigration
Lawyers; Editor: Stephen Yale-Loehr
Publisher: Matthew Bender and Company, Inc.

H-1B Handbook
Authors: Austin T. Fragomen Jr. and Steven C. Bell
Publisher: Thomson/West

Homeland Security Deskbook
Authors: Venable LLP; General Editor and Author of several
chapters: James O'Reilly
Publisher: Matthew Bender and Company, Inc.

Immigration Employment Compliance Handbook
Authors: Austin T. Fragomen Jr. and Steven C. Bell
Publisher: Thomson/West

Immigration Law and Business
Authors: Austin T. Fragomen Jr., Alfred J. Del Rey Jr., and

Sam Bernsen
Publisher: Thomson/West

Immigration Law and Crimes
Authors: Dan Kesselbrenner and Lory D. Rosenberg, under the
auspices of the National Immigration Project of the National
Lawyers Guild. December 2006 Update Editor: Jennifer Foster
Publisher: Thomson/West

Immigration Law and Defense
Author: National Immigration Project of the
National Lawyers Guild
Publisher: Thomson/West

Immigration Law and Health
Author: Sana Loue
Publisher: Thomson/West

Immigration Law and the Family
Authors: Sarah B. Ignatius and Elisabeth S. Stickney, under the aus-
pices of the National Immigration Project of the National Lawyers
Guild; 2004 Update Editor: Mary A. Kenney
Publisher: Thomson/West

Immigration Law Practice Expediter
Authors: Stanley Mailman and Stephen Yale-Loehr
Publisher: Matthew Bender and Company, Inc.

Immigration Law Service, 2nd ed.
Author: Anna Marie Gallagher
Publisher: Thomson/West

Immigration Legislation Handbook
Authors: Austin T. Fragomen Jr., Steven C. Bell, and
Thomas E. Moseley
Publisher: Thomson/West

Immigration Pleading and Practice Manual
Authors: Anna Marie Gallagher and Thomas Hutchins
Publisher: Thomson/West

Immigration Practice Manual
Publisher: Massachusetts Continuing Legal Education, Inc.

Immigration Procedures Handbook
Authors: Austin T. Fragomen Jr., Alfred J. Del Rey Jr. and
Steven C. Bell
Publisher: Thomson/West

*Kurzban's Immigration Law Sourcebook: A Comprehensive
Outline and Reference Tool,* Eleventh Edition
Author: Ira J. Kurzban
Publisher: American Immigration Lawyers Association

Labor Certification Handbook
Authors: Austin T. Fragomen Jr. and Steven C. Bell
Publisher: Thomson/West

Steel on Immigration Law, 2nd ed.
Author: Richard D. Steel
Publisher: Thomson/West

U.S. Citizenship and Naturalization Handbook
Authors: Daniel Levy; Update Editor: Charles Roth
Publisher: Thomson/West

Directories and Reference Materials
Encyclopedia of American Immigration
Editor: James Ciment
M. E. Sharpe, Inc. (2001)

A four-volume resource containing articles, essays, laws, and other
items relating to immigration.

Encyclopedia of North American Immigration
Author: John Powell
Facts on File, Inc. (2005)

A comprehensive source containing events, themes, people, places, and legislation related to immigration.

Immigration in America Today
Editors: James Loucky, Jeanne Armstrong, and Larry J. Estrada
Greenwood Publishing (2006)

A comprehensive resource on immigration-related issues.

Immigration: Library in a Book
Author: John Powell
Infobase Publishing (2007)

Includes an overview and history of immigration. Contains an instructive guide on immigration research and a bibliography of reference materials including books, articles, and films. Also contains a list of organizations and agencies that deal with immigration law.

Martindale-Hubbell website
http://www.martindale.com

Directory of law firms and lawyers. Searchable by geographic location and practice areas (including immigration).

Index

About the Author

A native of the Philippines, **Victor C. Romero** is the Maureen B. Cavanaugh Distinguished Faculty Scholar and Professor of Law at The Pennsylvania State University's Dickinson School of Law. He is author most recently of *Alienated: Immigrant Rights, the Constitution, and Equality in America* (New York University Press 2005).